THE INVESTIGATION

THE INVESTIGATION

A Former FBI Agent Uncovers the Truth Behind
Howard Hughes, Melvin Dummar and the
Most Contested Will in American History

GARY MAGNESEN

BARRICADE
BOOKS

Fort Lee • New Jersey

Published by Barricade Books Inc.
185 Bridge Plaza North
Suite 308-A
Fort Lee, NJ 07024

www.barricadebooks.com

Library of Congress Cataloging-in-Publication Data

Magnesen, Gary.
  The investigation : a former FBI agent uncovers the truth behind Howard
  Hughes, Melvin Dummar, and the most contested will in American history /
  Gary Magnesen.
    p. cm.
  ISBN 1-56980-294-7 (hc)
1. Hughes, Howard, 1905-1976--Will. 2. Wills--United States. 3. Forgery--
United States. 4. Dummar, Melvin--Trials, litigation, etc. 5. Hughes, Howard,
1905-1976--Estate. I. Title.

  KF759.H84M34 2005
  346.7305'4--dc22
                                                              2005053084

Second Printing
Printed in Canada

Contents

To those who willingly provided the truth.

Acknowledgments

I owe this book to my brother, Dean, and his wife, Jennie, who challenged me to begin this project. Without their joint support this book wouldn't exist.

Other members of my wonderful family also were instrumental in this project. Greg, Kristi and Adrienne helped me shape this book and made critical readings of the manuscript. Jill skillfully prepared the artist's conception of Howard Hughes. Dave, Steve, Leslie, Heather, Caryn, and Robert provided invaluable encouragement and energy.

I also want to thank my former FBI associates, Dennis Arnoldy, and Jerry Doherty for their help. Walter Bode helped me shape this story into a readable tale and stretched my horizon while John L. Smith saw the potential for this investigative account. Publisher, Lyle Stuart, was kind enough to give the book the attention it needed and gave me hope.

I also want to thank all the people I interviewed who were so candid in providing information and insight. Robert Deiro showed remarkable courage in coming forward after all these years.

No one took a greater interest nor provided more encouragement than my wife, Diane. This book could never have been completed without her love and constant enlightened support.

Prologue

'm not some naive amateur. I've dealt with crooks, con men, and phonies most of my adult life. I lived the investigative experiences depicted in the hit movie *Casino*. I retired from the FBI in Las Vegas in May of 1996 after nearly twenty-six years of service as a special agent. I've dealt with mobsters, thieves, frauds, murderers, kidnappers, and drug dealers. They're all the same—they want something for nothing. They all feed off society, and the only difference among them is their varying levels of sophistication.

• • •

The kitchen seemed so small. I felt like I was being crushed by the size of it. An overwhelming sense of frustration and anger constricted my airway as I looked down at the pool of blood on the gray linoleum floor. The blood was thick like syrup and was beginning to congeal. It looked like someone had accidentally spilled a half gallon of the liquid. It had only been thirty minutes or so since the shooting, and emotions were bubbling over. I continued staring at the puddle and whispered to another agent in a raspy voice, "No one could survive after losing that much blood."

The night before, two Chicago police officers had attempted to take a burglary suspect into custody in a neighborhood bar on a cold winter afternoon, but the burglar had overpowered one of the cops and had managed to disarm him. He shot both officers dead and escaped.

The police determined that the burglar had a girlfriend who had recently moved into an apartment in Milwaukee. The police called the Milwaukee FBI office and requested that the apartment be checked out to determine if the fugitive was hiding there. Five agents from the bank robbery-fugitive squad responded. Two of them went to the rear of the apartment house and the others went into the four-story building through the front door. They went to the third floor and knocked on the door of the apartment just below the girlfriend's residence. They entered the dwelling and listened for any noise coming from the apartment above, but they couldn't hear anything. One of the agents walked to the kitchen and peered out the back door onto the rear external stairway. He opened the door and was immediately shot in the upper chest.

The force of the .38 caliber slug knocked him back into the kitchen. The bullet struck his collarbone and ricocheted downward inside his chest. As he lay there bleeding out, the wanted man ran down the wooden stairs holding a pistol in each hand. The agents at the rear of the complex responded immediately and rushed the stairs. There was a shoot-out, and one blast from a shotgun blew off part of the fugitive's left hand. He staggered momentarily but escaped around the corner of the building. He was pursued by the agents as they tracked his blood spots in the snow. Finally he was located inside a house a few blocks away, but he had taken a fourteen-year-old boy as a hostage. He demanded a getaway car, and it was provided. As he came out, he was holding a gun to the boy's temple. An agent positioned on the roof of a neighboring house shot the punk in the neck as the boy slipped on a patch of ice.

I was assigned control of the crime scene investigation, and as I stood in the kitchen staring at the blood, I was informed that the shooter was dead and the agent had miraculously survived. After we completed our job, I drove home. I had to get my shoes off. The soles were soaked in blood—a brother agent's blood. I would never wear those shoes again. That day, I lost my innocence as an agent. This wasn't a pretend world of cops and robbers—this was real. People kill people, and you never know when it might happen.

I was transferred to Las Vegas in October of 1980. I arrived after successfully completing an investigation of the Milwaukee La Cosa Nostra (Mafia) family. I was the case agent responsible for the investigation. The boss, Frank Balistrieri, had operated under law enforcement's radar for many years. I went to the head of the Milwaukee police department's intelligence unit to discuss joint cooperation, but he treated me condescendingly, as if I were a foolish schoolboy. After his verbal pat on the head, I knew he would eventually eat his demeaning words.

The investigation had been long and arduous, but with the collaborative efforts of two other agents who did a remarkable job, we brought down Frank Balistrieri and his whole crew. We had monitored conversations over wiretaps and strategically placed microphones for over a year. At times we had as many as thirty agents assisting on the case. We had overheard bits and pieces of evidence, but we weren't able to put all the puzzle pieces together. Information was finally received that the boss of the family had a secret office in a guarded building.

I was convinced we had to get a bug in that office. Armed with a court authorized break and enter order, we conducted a black bag job on the building. A Bureau lock-pick expert got us into the place, and we surreptitiously entered the basement. We had blueprints and took careful measurements until we were sure we were just below the office. We drilled through the thirteen-inch cement ceiling into the first floor. The drill was very quiet, but our senses were amplified by adrenaline. It sounded like a jackhammer. I wondered how the guard could miss the sound. The microphone was pushed up into the hole and we left.

The next day we began monitoring, but we only heard footsteps. We had missed by six inches and had placed the bug in a hallway outside the office. We had to go back in the next night and do it all over again. It wasn't a pleasant thought, but we had no choice. This time we hit the target. Over time, we began hearing cryptic conversations about monthly "transfusions." We eventually broke the code and learned that transfusions referred to the boss's share of skimming profits from Las Vegas casinos. Difficult investigations are often like that. You have to keep plugging away and adjusting your strategy until you have the answers you need.

I've met the people of Las Vegas. My career as an FBI agent has taken me on an inside tour of the city. As the organized crime program coordinator for the Las Vegas field office, I worked the underbelly of the sprawling place for sixteen years. I remember meeting a top-heavy dominatrix who looked like a flamingo. Her thin legs held up her unbelievable chest. She lived with other women who slithered in and out of view as my partner and I interviewed her. Her skin was like coarse leather, her face the shape and texture of a first baseman's glove. The glove had been rubbed with moisturizing lotion, but it didn't penetrate the leather; it just coated it. It wasn't possible to determine how old she was, but she had seen her best days. The house reeked of cheap perfume and talcum powder. After the interview, she excitedly offered to show us her dungeon. How could we refuse her offer?

The room was apart from the main living area. It was equipped with shackles, chains, ropes, pulleys, a four-foot high wooden stock, and several leather whips. She explained the various uses of the implements, and as I listened my stomach began to turn. There were spots on the carpet and on the walls. They had the appearance of rust. I assumed they were blood.

She was almost giddy as she talked. I had to get out of the place. As we left I noticed a doghouse and a collar on a chain. I naively asked, "Where's your dog?"

She giggled, "Oh, that's not for a dog. That's for a client. He comes over every week, and I chain him up and feed him dog food. He usually stays for a few hours. He pays well."

That did it for me. The woman was creepy. I felt like I needed a shower. When we got back in the car, my partner and I couldn't stop our nervous laughter.

I remember a cab driver who was a loan shark victim. He earned pretty good money, but he lived in a small hovel. I was struck with the totally barren, single room studio apartment. He had a mattress on the floor and a small TV. That was it, except for a pile of dirty clothes discarded in a corner. There was a pot of something on the stove. A surprisingly pleasant odor filled the tiny room. I didn't see any dishes. I assumed he ate directly out of the pot. The man was a degenerate gambler, a horse bettor, the worst kind. When he received a few bucks in tips he would rush to the race book and lay it down on a horse. In order to survive he borrowed from loan sharks. He borrowed from one to pay another. Now he was in trouble. The short, squat, broken man had been roughed up by his creditors, and he had come running to us for help.

There was a washed-up showgirl who adorned her home's pink walls with nude photos of herself. Her pancake makeup looked painted on. She wore candy-apple red lipstick, and her eyes were black from the flapping of her fake eyelashes. The carpet was purple; the drapes were red. I felt I was in a circus tent in the presence of a pitiful clown. She had been the girlfriend of an old mobster years ago, and she wanted to share stories of the good old days.

I've been in the rambling house of a strip club owner. The house was full of voluptuous nude statues. There were sixteen bedrooms and ten baths in the single man's house. He was a Greek immigrant who had found his American dream.

I've been in a zero star motel room of a woman and her three children. She had two little girls. One looked to be three and the other was probably five. The boy was about eight or nine. His young eyes already reflected despair. The woman's husband had been arrested on a dope charge, and there was no food in the place. The family had nowhere to turn. It was a barren room, a lonely place. There were no toys, no signs of permanency. I was there to ask her about her husband's activities, but all she could do was cry. She had no hope. I saw my children in her children's faces, so I did what I had to do. I bought some food for the family and paid twenty-nine dollars for another day's rent. I don't know what happened to them. I hope she took my advice and escaped to a shelter.

I have chased a fugitive through 1950s-era, small, square multi-colored houses. One was pink, one yellow, and another purple. We found the man hiding in a closet inside the purple house. The place had been used as a toilet by the family pit bull. The droppings were like land mines spread out on the floor. There was a toddler in the house, alone.

I've been in the palatial mansions of nouveau riche bankers, lawyers, and casino executives. All of the homes were tastefully decorated and comfortable. I've sat in squalid mobile homes. I've toured the ranch of a wealthy ex-state senator who bragged about his expensive quarter horses. Animals he had purchased with bribe money. He strutted around in his hand-sewn ostrich cowboy boots and Wrangler jeans held up by a silver-buckled belt. His white Stetson hat proclaimed to the world, "I'm a good guy." But he wasn't. He was dark and corrupt, a miserable excuse for a public official.

I've sat in the homes of ordinary people who work hard and live their lives like regular folks. They have neighborhood parties and barbecues, and they help one another. They bring dinner in when their neighbors are sick, and they baby-sit each others' children. They take their children to Cub Scouts, soccer practice, and dance lessons. They attend football games to watch their sons live out their dreams.

Las Vegas is two towns. The "strip," lined with casinos, lights, and glitter, is a plastic world of make-believe.

Residents, who for better or worse, live their lives in the other world.

The once dusty, rowdy town is now a corporate enclave, controlled by accountants and gaming officials. It produces thousands of service jobs and is marketed like an adult Disneyland. The current marketing slogan is, "What happens in Las Vegas—stays in Las Vegas." Since 1980 the population of the area has doubled to a million people, and it's predicted to double again in the next ten years.

After the mob control of Las Vegas was broken, adventurous mobsters continued to move to Sin City. They weren't seeking hidden ownership of casinos but were drawn there like most tourists, for the weather and the excitement of the town. Most of these guys were members of various New York City La Cosa Nostra families, and had taken the oath of silence known as "Omerta." This code required them to swear allegiance to the family and to commit crimes, including murder. When we learned that these wise guys were residents in Vegas, we began looking at them. It was great fun and a supreme challenge. As an FBI agent I had learned that there is no hunting like the hunting of a man. That was our mission—to take them down, one at a time, by finding a crime to charge them with. They had joined a secret criminal enterprise, and as soon as they did, they became fair game for federal prosecution.

Most of the guys were older mobsters—old school, low profile. They had their hooks into long-standing criminal businesses on the East Coast. They controlled their operations long distance. One, Natale Richichi, a Gambino family capo (captain) controlled pornography in New England. Another, Charlie (Moose) Panarella, a Colombo family capo, received kickbacks from New York City unions and other enterprises. John Mascia, a Gambino soldier, supplied slot machines to illegal gambling operations in New York. John Conti, a Luchese family soldier, pulled wire fraud scams. Fat Stevie Cino, a Buffalo, New York family soldier, was involved in all sorts of crimes, and Vito DeFilippo, a Bonanno family capo, exercised power over Las Vegas strip joints.

There were many others. Suffice it to say—when these guys popped their heads up, I went after them.

Yet some remnants of the past remain. The incumbent mayor of Las Vegas, a former mob attorney who represented some of those we arrested, has taken a pause from his criminal defense practice. He once stated publicly that he would rather have his daughter marry a mobster than an FBI agent.

• • •

Conducting investigations has been my life's work as some of my "war stories" attest. My experiences on the street have made me a skeptic when it comes to human behavior. The truth about an individual is often hidden behind a mask. A good investigator peels back the layers of the disguise to find the real person.

I met Melvin Dummar in the summer of 2002. He had worked as an electronics salesman for my brother off and on for many years. My brother recommended that I talk to Melvin and get his side of the Howard Hughes story as it had never been told effectively. He suggested it would give me something interesting to do in my retirement, and it would stretch my investigative muscles again. Besides, it would be an interesting and unique challenge. I have to admit that prior to meeting Melvin, I had come into this with some bias. I had the impression he was a kook. This was based on media reports, and my understanding that his story was on the same magnitude as someone claiming to have been abducted by aliens. I had no idea if he had forged Howard Hughes's will or not. It seemed logical to assume that he had, as he had been named as an implausible beneficiary in the will. Why would Howard Hughes name someone like Dummar in his will? It didn't make any sense to me.

When I met Melvin Dummar, he asked me to look into the facts and conduct my own investigation of the will and his improbable story. When I asked him why he was opening the old wounds again, he responded passionately, "I just want people to respect me. I want them to know that I'm not a fraud or a crook. My reputation means more to me than money or any other thing. I want my family to know that I was helping someone in need when I picked up the old man in the desert. I wasn't sure if I could believe him when he said he was Howard Hughes, and to be honest, I didn't think much more about it until the day the will was delivered to me. It changed my life, it ruined it, cost me thousands of dollars, and it cost me my friends and my reputation."

I asked him, "It's been thirty-eight years since all this happened. What do you want to accomplish by an investigation after all these years?"

"I just want to clear the air and have someone tell the story from my point of view. Everybody involved has told the story from their side, but I've been quiet all these years."

At first glance, this was another Las Vegas story, a con job, a get-rich scheme, but I consented to make some inquiries, at my own expense, as Dummar couldn't afford me. Besides, it could be interesting and a unique challenge. I'd do a couple of interviews and maybe look at some documents, and that should do it. Hopefully, my training and intuition, honed by years of experience at looking behind masks, would help me penetrate Dummar's façade. I was sure that when I unmasked Dummar, I would find the face of a charlatan.

Usually there is a hint, although slight, of deception when crooks are interrogated. The eyes, the body language, the throbbing veins of the neck can tell a story. Are the answers direct, or is it obvious the wheels are turning to find a convincing answer. In the end, a good investigator develops an intuition, a sense of who is telling the truth and who isn't. I also have a degree in psychology, which is often useful. This is by no means a perfect sense, but more often than not it leads in the right investigative direction.

1

Meet Melvin Dummar

*"I'm telling you, Howard Hughes never left the confines
of his suite in the Desert Inn Hotel while he lived in Las
Vegas! Since he didn't leave, he couldn't have been in
the desert, and since he wasn't in the desert, Melvin
Dummar couldn't have picked him up."*
—*Kay Glenn, Hughes insider*

Melvin Dummar is a common man, a blade of grass in
the vast meadow of humanity. He's much like millions
of other men, a face in the crowd, a name on an endless list of names. Or is he a charlatan and con man? I had
to find out for myself.

Melvin Dummar has driven the back roads of life from
his earliest years. These roads have taken him through deep
eroded gullies and to the tops of majestic mesas. Like many
others, he has slipped off the road countless times, but to
this day he continues to seek a smooth highway for his life.

Melvin was born in the vermilion canyon country of
southern Utah in 1944. His mother lived in Springdale, a
quaint tourist town at the mouth of Zion National Park. His
father was away serving in the Navy during World War II

when Melvin was born. After his release from the service, Arnold chased work to Felspar, Nevada. Times were hard after the war, and Arnold found employment in a mine. Felspar no longer exists. Like many mining towns, it has disappeared off the face of the earth. The mining dried up and the town died. There are no buildings left; only dust remains.

Melvin was the fourth of ten children, six boys and four girls. His oldest sister, Mary Ellen, fell into a mineshaft as a child and died before Melvin was born. Another sister recently died of cancer. Not long after I met Melvin, his brother, Jess, was stabbed to death as he got off a bus in Salt Lake City. The crime remains unsolved. Another brother owns a small café and other businesses in Gabbs, NV, and has served as mayor of the town.

The Dummar family moved to Fallon, Nevada in 1947 where Arnold found much needed construction work on a road crew. The young Melvin viewed the move to Fallon as an adventure. He was too young to notice that Fallon was not as scenic as Springdale. At the age of eight or nine he remembers finding a ten dollar bill. He used it to buy a Daisy BB gun.

He had a passion for running the hills around Fallon, shooting his "pea shooter." When he was thirteen, even though money was tight, his mother bought him a .22 caliber rifle. He enjoyed hunting rabbits and varmints in the desert. The wilds of Nevada became part of Melvin. The Joshua tree cacti, with their sword-shaped spears, and the scrub-covered hillsides became his playground. He loves the open country of Nevada to this day. He avoids big cities and large crowds.

The Nevada sun is relentless, but the stifling heat had no affect on the young Melvin. He was happiest when he went out alone. He considered the high desert his, and he only shared it willingly with the lizards and snakes. He had a few friends, but they didn't share his passion for the desert.

His family moved to Bellflower, California and then returned near Fallon, to Gabbs, Nevada. Melvin was unsettled. He was always looking for something—a brass ring that would bring him what he wanted. He broke away from his family and moved back and forth between California and Nevada several times. By the time he graduated from Long Beach High School, he had honed his musical skills. His father described Melvin as his most sensitive child. He said he had a gift for music.

Melvin recalls singing at various churches at a very early age. He told me he attended the Mormon Church sporadically, but "I went to whatever church the prettiest girls attended." He says he has many notebook binders filled with his musical compositions. Periodically, he withdrew to the solitude of his music. It was a soothing balm to his soul. He often sat for hours writing songs. He found that he had a talent for country western music. He felt he could speak through his music. His gentle tenor voice expressed his deepest feelings. He even had a few gigs in local bars. Some were paid performances but most were informal presentations. He was happiest when performing or writing songs. It took him to a different world—his world. It's been said that country music is "... five chords and the truth." The lyrics of his music told stories of his dreams and of his everyday cares and hopes. He wrote songs like "Dreams Can Become a Reality," "Get Back Devil, Leave Me Alone," "I Took a Peek Through Heaven's Door," and "I Found a Rose." One of his favorite lines is "... Find a yellow rose, and give it to the one you adore, and you will be happy forever..."

He performed a cabaret act in a Reno, Nevada casino in 1979 for a few days. He was dressed in a Las Vegas-style satin body suit and was backed up by a small band and two dancing girls arrayed in colored ostrich feathers. His stint at the club was not renewed. His dream to become a country western singer has now faded with time.

While living in California, Melvin got hooked on TV game shows. He set out to become a contestant on various programs that required dressing up in nutty costumes and acting like some mindless fool. I wondered if he had weaved a grand conspiracy to get Hughes's money in furtherance of his hope that, "Dreams Can Become a Reality."

Melvin enlisted in the Air Force in 1963, but he was discharged after nine months because of his "emotional make-up." He explained that he was extremely immature at the time and had been involved with a girl who sent him a "Dear John" letter, and he couldn't deal with it. The Air Force determined that he was emotionally immature and discharged him. After that failed relationship, and after two disastrous marriages to his former wife, Linda, he discovered that there were only two things to do in Gabbs. He worked hard, and he dreamed. He dreamed of being a singer, and he dreamed of clapping fans reacting to his music. His dream was an escape from his bonds even when filling bags with powdered magnesium while working at the Gabbs mine. He believed that with hard work and a little luck he could succeed as an entertainer. I wondered if he rationalized that "Dreams Can Become a Reality" permitted him to commit fraud.

Melvin has always been emotional. It's probably the driving force of his creativity, but it also has a downside. He has often been directed by his heart instead of his head. Some of his life's decisions have been flawed. Many of his choices have been bad, and life has dealt him a poor hand many times. In spite of this, he has worked hard to support his family.

He has worked at a number of jobs, never satisfied with the results. The money was never enough. He has worked in a mine, as a milkman, a beer truck driver, an electronics salesman, and has operated his own gas station. Nowadays, when his health permits, he loads a chest freezer with meat bought from a local butcher and heads to the rural parts of western Nevada. The freezer is powered by a gas generator and sits in the back of his white Chevy pickup truck. He has many loyal customers, many of them widows, who live miles from the nearest grocery store. He has found a unique market niche for a man who is willing to pay the price of long hours on the road. When I asked him how his meat business was doing he responded, "I do all right."

Melvin's eyes tell much about him. They twinkle with optimism, but they are also deep blue somber reservoirs. I wondered what secrets his eyes had seen.

He has some stains on his history. He's been arrested three times. He was arrested once for forgery in 1967 and once for shoplifting in 1970. He was also arrested for buying stolen guns while living in Willard, Utah. All of the charges were dismissed.

The forgery arrest occurred in Gabbs, where he was charged with forging and cashing a payroll check. A female bartender identified him as the perpetrator, and the charges ended in a hung jury.

The shoplifting charge was a strange one. Melvin had been installing a soap dish in his home on a Sunday, but the screws weren't long enough. He decided to go to a grocery store, the only open store in town, and found a small plastic box of various sized screws. He opened the box to determine the length of the screws. He brought the two original screws with him for comparison. He found that the boxed screws were not long enough and returned them to the shelf. He was arrested for having two screws in his pocket. The charges were eventually dropped.

The gun charge stemmed from a young man offering Melvin some rifles for sale. He had said that his grandfather had left the guns to him. Melvin bought the rifles and was arrested for buying stolen property. A judge in the wrong county signed the search warrant for Melvin's residence. The search was thrown out, and the charges were dropped.

Melvin's body turned on him in 2002. He had been healthy all his life, but his cells developed cancer, grew in his stomach, and spread to his lymphatic system. He was very sick. Melvin underwent a radical chemotherapy regimen at the University of Utah Cancer Center. His malignant cancer cells were bombarded with anticancer drugs. These drugs attack the cancer cells and essentially poison them to death. Unfortunately, these same drugs poison normal cells as well, particularly the rapidly dividing cells of the body such as bone marrow, intestinal linings, hair follicles, and the cells of the mouth. His hair fell out; he was constantly nauseated and couldn't eat because his small intestines rejected the food. The doctors drilled into his femur bone and withdrew some of his bone marrow to treat it in an effort to finish off any remaining cancer cells. Then it was frozen and placed in a freezer for storage. They killed his remaining bone marrow and injected the treated marrow back into his bones. In spite of medicine's remarkable progress in cancer treatment, this almost seems like a throwback to eighteenth century medicine and the days of bleeding a patient to empty the body of its impurities.

Melvin was quarantined for five weeks while his treated bone marrow began producing new white blood cells, the body's infection fighters. During the five-week confinement in solitary, he had to be guarded against infection, as his body had no capacity to fight on its own. This procedure is used only in the treatment of potentially fatal disorders, but in spite of the chamber of horrors and medical torture, his cancer is currently in remission. He tires easily and has his up days and his down days, so he is unable to work full time. The threat of recurrence hangs over his life like a guillotine. The blade could drop at any time. In spite of his health, he believes in the future. His philosophy of life is short and succinct. He says, "Things will be better tomorrow."

Melvin was sublimely optimistic and showed me a degree of class and strength that surprised and impressed me. He was looking death in the face, yet he held to his story. Melvin clearly loves his family and works hard, even in his weakened condition. I asked myself, what if life had a grudge against Melvin? What if he were telling the truth? If not, why would he willingly rip open an old sore? Either he was a phony or the ultimate victim. I considered the remote possibility that Melvin was telling the truth. If he were telling the truth, then he had been forced to drink from a bitter cup of scorn and had been victimized in the extreme. Justice had been dashed to bits—a fortune had been snatched from him, and then as a final stroke of the lash, he was forever branded as a crook and an idiot.

I didn't want to be the source of another unfulfilled dream. How could I turn him down? Besides, Melvin has danced to his own music most of his life, and this may be his last dance.

I would do a little investigation at my own expense, as Melvin couldn't afford me. I'd do a couple of interviews and maybe look at some documents, and that should do it. I wasn't certain that Melvin was being straight with me. Either he was a masterful con artist, or he was being truthful.

Why would Melvin reopen Pandora's box of nightmares after all these years if he wasn't sincere about his motives? There is no present legal recourse for him. The statute of limitations on the Hughes matter has long since run out. The whole unpleasant business would be revived, and more mockery of Melvin would result if I found that he was lying. He had nothing to gain but a rehabilitated reputation. Maybe, with his illness, he has a renewed sense of his own mortality and wants to set the record straight.

• • •

I've worked cold cases before, but this one was frozen, buried, and forgotten. It was doubtful that any forensic evidence would exist after thirty-five years. There would be no footprints in the dirt road. There would be no blood. There would be no tire tracks, and many potential witnesses would be dead. I would probably have to be satisfied with reviewing depositions and trial transcripts of witnesses. This would be a case of examining old records, research, and hopefully developing a living witness somewhere, somehow. Without FBI credentials, I'd be much like a beggar with an outstretched tin cup, relying on the cooperation of strangers in this investigation.

As I returned home from interviewing Melvin, my thoughts wandered to a time when I had come across a man I'll call "Big Tony." He claimed he knew several people who were mobbed up in Las Vegas. His assertions seemed too good to be true. Many of my fellow agents discounted his statements as they felt he was "blowing hot air." They felt he was trying to ingratiate himself with the FBI and was inflating his abilities. I was skeptical of him at first, but after looking into several of his claims, I came to believe him. His stories checked out. In the real world of investigations, corroboration of information is the only way to determine the reliability of a witness. Time and again his information was right on the mark.

Big Tony opened a social club, and his associates flocked to the place. He hosted nightly meals where various scufflers could hang out while the linguini and clam sauce simmered and the wine chilled. The mob guys told stories, made criminal admissions, and schemes were hatched. It was all recorded by strategically placed FBI microphones. We had difficulty keeping up with all the crimes discussed by the motley group. In the end we solved numerous crimes, including a murder, armed robberies, and much more. I wondered if I would be able to corroborate any of Melvin's tale, or if it was just a fantastic story told by a man seeking fame and riches.

2

The Desert Inn

In 1905 an early ramshackle community became the fledgling city of Las Vegas. It was a dusty, rough, and raw town inhabited by many cunning and independent men. Men who wouldn't give an inch for what they believed in or what they wanted. While the northern cow counties have essentially remained the same, a revolutionary transformation occurred in the south. Gambling was legalized in 1931 but the town remained a dusty railroad stop where poker and primitive slot machines could be played. The taxes from gaming revenues kept the city alive.

Coincidentally, in the same year, construction began on the 726-foot high Hoover Dam. This masterpiece of human creation is implanted in the deep, narrow Black Canyon Gorge. It is a fan shaped, concrete barrier, an out-thrust shield, holding back the force of the Colorado River. Lake Mead supplies water for the unquenchable thirst of Las Vegas, and the hydroelectric power produced by the huge turbines allowed for the use of an innovative device called an air conditioner. Now, the city known for its oppressive, stifling heat could be tamed.

Casinos replaced the dark taverns of the past, and investments trickled into the city. Legal gambling was new in Nevada. It had always been illegal in other parts of the United States, but there were experts in the art of gambling just as there had been experts in the art of booze making during Prohibition. These experts flocked to the new gaming Mecca, as did their money. Many of these gamblers were part of organized crime. It was a natural evolution of things. They knew how to run a game and they knew how to ensure profits.

The local good ole boys weren't so sophisticated, so they did what was natural for them—they took advantage of the new industry. This arrangement satisfied both sides. There were no range wars in the South over gambling, but to succeed you had to be on the inside of one of the two prominent groups—the gamblers or the good ole boys. This inside connection is referred to as "juice." In order to get a good job you had to be juiced in. In order to build a casino you were required to be juiced in. Gaming control by the state was nearly nonexistent. It was a laissez-faire world. When Howard Hughes came to town in 1966, he was juiced in by the "good ole boys." They saw his entrance into the casino business as a way of erasing the influence of organized crime and legitimizing Las Vegas to the rest of the country. Hughes bought several casinos controlled by organized crime elements.

• • •

Howard Hughes often wandered through the Las Vegas casinos alone, dressed in a rumpled seersucker suit, open collared shirt, and canvas sneakers. "He looked like a derelict," said a veteran gambler. "I met him in the men's room one time. He was washing a spot off his shirt. I thought he was a bum doing his laundry in the sink. Somebody said, 'That's Howard Hughes.' I asked, 'Who the hell is Howard Hughes?'"

Years later, a truck loaded with luggage, several sedans, and a station wagon converted into an ambulance drove slowly south on Las Vegas Boulevard. Their destination was the Desert Inn Hotel and Casino. A man using the alias of Robert Murphy had made all of the arrangements. He'd rented the entire ninth floor of the Desert Inn in the name of Jack Trent. The doorknobs had been removed from the doors leading to the two fire stairwells between floors, and the elevator was fixed so it wouldn't go to the ninth floor without a special key. Two secure phone lines had been connected, as had two television sets. A special air filter was installed to filter out dust and germs to the entire floor.

It was 4:15 in the morning of November 27, 1966. This is the time known as the dead zone in casinos, as most of the gamblers have had enough and have gone to bed. It's the time the casinos almost come to a standstill while cleaning crews vacuum and scrub everything, and the count crews empty the slot machines of the winnings. They fill buckets with nickels, quarters, and dollar tokens and take them to the hard count room. This is where thousands of dollars in change are weighed, wrapped, and prepared for deposit. A few die-hard gamblers remain in the casinos, but not many.

The eight men guarding the station wagon opened the side door to the building and, with some effort, lifted a stretcher from the vehicle. The man who, in the past, had wandered the casinos in his seersucker suit was now dressed in blue pajamas. He lay motionless, and looked to be dead as they carried him up the nine flights of the fire escape stairwell to the penthouse. Howard Hughes had returned to Sin City.

• • •

Howard Robard Hughes was born in Houston, Texas in 1905. He was the only child of Howard Hughes, Sr. and Allene Gano Hughes. Hughes showed signs of a high intellect early in life and was an adventurer. This was probably a form of rebellion against his mother's suffocating attention. He took flying lessons at the age of fourteen and fell in love with aviation and airplanes.

In 1932, he founded Hughes Aircraft Corporation and designed and constructed airplanes for commercial and military use. World War II increased the need for more military aircraft, and Hughes helped supply that need. Another of his companies, Hughes Electronics, was one of the largest suppliers of weapons to the Air Force and Navy. He was instrumental in supplying weapons that led to victory in World War II. In the 1960s, the company helped develop space satellites.

Hughes left Houston and moved to Hollywood, where he produced approximately forty movies. He was six foot four, slim, and considered handsome, rivaling many of the leading men of the day. He was a notorious womanizer and bedded one movie starlet after another. He also kept several young, hopeful starlets in apartments all over Los Angeles as if they were his personal collection.

He had several medical problems, including being hard of hearing, from an early age. This caused him to do much of his business over the telephone, as he could hear better over the phone. It is said that he contracted syphilis as a young man. He was involved in fourteen airplane and automobile crashes over the years, one resulting in the death of a pedestrian. His high risk test pilot days resulted in several crashes leaving him with massive injuries.

Because of the constant pain, he became addicted to

painkillers and later developed what we understand today as obsessive-compulsive disorder. His germ phobia increased, and in his later years he retreated to his bedroom where he sat naked all day, turning out endless pages of handwritten memos. He kept the blinds pulled shut, watching his precious movie productions and eating candy bars, soup, and ice cream. He seldom ate properly, and his health began to deteriorate.

At his prime, Hughes was the richest man in America, having accumulated a financial empire worth two and a half billion dollars. This fortune, figured for inflation today, would be close to eight billion dollars. Hughes was the Bill Gates of his day when it came to personal wealth.

Hughes married actress Jean Peters in 1957. They had lived in California, but the marriage was a strange one. To show Peters his independence, Hughes had personally driven her to their new home. This was very unusual, as he was usually chauffeured at that point in time. Hughes treated her as a prize and not as a wife. Hughes often did things that seemed irrational, and for unknown reasons he left his wife in July of 1966.

According to an aide, Hughes became a nudist because his clothes reeked of stale body odor. He said, "We couldn't touch the doorknobs. We couldn't touch his telephone or his Kleenex boxes. We couldn't touch his writing pads or his pens." He went on to explain that they would bring Hughes three copies of the same newspapers and he would reach out with a Kleenex-covered hand and pull the middle paper out. One of the aides would bring Hughes his lunch in a paper bag. "The bag would be held at a forty-five degree angle from his body, and Hughes would take a Kleenex, reach into the bag, and pull out the contents one by one…"

Hughes moved to Boston for a time in 1966 to get special medical treatment, and then he took a chartered train to Las Vegas. It's believed he was too ill to fly. He told an aide, "I don't want to fly on my back like some stiff."

With the assistance of Bob Maheu, Hughes began buying up casinos. Maheu had used the name Robert Murphy in setting up arrangements for Mr. Hughes's arrival in Las Vegas. The management of the Desert Inn started to become nervous because the high rollers—their very best and richest customers—had no special place to stay at the Desert Inn as the entire ninth floor, known as the penthouse suites, was occupied by Hughes and his staff. He refused to move out, and quite a struggle ensued. Finally, Hughes ordered Maheu to buy the hotel. He gave instructions to pay whatever the owners wanted for the place because he was not moving.

My research shows that Hughes bought the Desert Inn for $13.25 million on March 3, 1967. Four months later he bought the Sands Casino for twenty-three million dollars.

The Sands Hotel and Casino was the hang-out of Frank Sinatra and his so-called rat pack. The whole pack were regulars at the Sands. They all performed there. Sinatra owned nine percent of the facility, but he acted as if he ran the place. He was very rude and demanding. When Mr. Hughes bought the Sands, he gave instructions that Frank Sinatra's gambling credit line be canceled. When Sinatra learned of this, he became enraged. He threw a tantrum. He threw chips and yelled profanities and made a complete fool of himself. He went looking for the casino manager. He found him having lunch in the coffee shop and approached him in a rage. Sinatra yelled that Hughes couldn't do this to him, and that he had built the hotel from a sandpile. Then he overturned the dining table on the man. The casino manager was a reasonable man, but he also weighed 275 pounds, and he punched Sinatra in the mouth, knocking out two of his teeth and laying him flat on his back. Howard Hughes had clearly taken control of Las Vegas.

• • •

Looking at Las Vegas now I wonder if the disembodied spirit of Howard Hughes hovers over the city, pleased with what the city has become. A land developer who knows Hughes's Las Vegas history has said, "Hughes had a gift. He could see into the future. He was like a visionary. He had a huge master plan for this town."

Hughes saw Las Vegas as a hub of commerce. He foresaw a supersonic airport built outside the city to accommodate jumbo jets. He saw people commuting from the airport by helicopter and landing on helipads on the roofs of hotels. He saw extravagant hotels, palaces of pleasure, where every need would be met. He saw the finest restaurants in the world, home to world-renowned chefs. He saw endless tracts of homes, spread across the valley. Homes built on land that was nothing but raw, gray desert. He put the $546,549,771 he made from the sale of TWA to work for him in Vegas. He bought twenty-five thousand acres of land from the Union Pacific Railroad. He stole it for $2.50 an acre. The land now goes for two hundred and eighty thousand dollars an acre. He understood that the acreage would appreciate in value over time. Like gold, its value is based on finite reserves. In 1966, there were two hundred thousand people in the city. Today, there are one million. Remaining building lots are at a premium with the phenomenal growth of the city. Nevada, thanks to Las Vegas, has been the fastest growing state in the nation for eighteen years in a row.

Hughes bought thousands of additional acres east and west of the Tonopah Highway. Houses now fill the desert void all the way to the mountains. He purchased numerous mansions for his executives. He bought seven casinos and KLAS-TV. The television station cost him $3,650,000. He took over Alamo Airways and the Thunderbird Field, plus four hundred acres in North Las Vegas. He paid four million dollars for them. An old-timer speculated, "He's buying up the competition. They don't stand a chance against this guy. He's like a bulldozer. With his bankroll—he plows down everything in his way. He's buying up the whole place."

Another veteran Las Vegan spoke admirably of the entrepreneur, "He knew everything about this town. It was like he had lived here all his life."

When Hughes bought several hundred acres on the strip for three million dollars, another local groused, "He'll own the whole damn place before long. He'll be like a king. We'll all be his servants."

Hughes obtained the vast expanse of the Spring Valley Ranch and adjacent rangeland, forty-five minutes north of the city. Thousands of head of cattle would supply Las Vegas with prime beef for its posh restaurants. The visionary was well on his way to controlling every aspect of the city's economy.

Nevada law requires a complete background investigation on any prospective casino buyer as well as key employees of casinos. This is to ensure a clean gaming industry. Complete financial reviews are made and associates are vetted to determine undue influence by organized crime or by other unseemly characters. This is normally a painstaking process involving volumes of written applications, but for Hughes it was a simple matter. His one-page application provided his name, age, and a brief physical description. The casinos were purchased in the name of Hughes Tool Company for which Hughes was the sole owner. The Nevada Gaming Control Board (NGCB) is the investigative arm for the Nevada Gaming Commission, a panel of political appointees who determine suitability for licensing. A member of the NGCB recommended licensing because, "After all, Mr. Hughes's life and background are well known to this board, and we consider him to be highly qualified."

After this announcement, an investigator was heard to say, "Everybody knew what happened with his license. Hughes bought it, just like he buys everything else."

I stumbled across evidence that this statement was in all likelihood true. Hughes bought his first casino in March of 1967—that same month, he purchased gold mines near Virginia City. The sellers of these mines were Eldon Cleveland and a partner. They had acquired the spent mines by quitclaim deed for five hundred dollars, two days before they sold the mines to Hughes Tool Company for two hundred and twenty-five thousand dollars. This deal appeared to be an ordinary scam until I realized that the partner was a member of the Nevada Gaming Commission who had voted to approve Hughes for licensing. I wonder how many other deals remain submerged in the muck of this political swamp?

A bagman named LeVane Forsythe has admitted to passing envelopes to various officials and politicians on behalf of Hughes. He has boasted, "I passed a package to Don Nixon, the President's brother." Then he added slyly, "It was a loan."

Another courier has admitted to delivering three bulky envelopes on behalf of Hughes in December of 1967. He explained, "I don't know what was in the envelopes, but it was probably grease to take care of a squeak."

Hughes had other allies in Sin City. Hank Greenspun, the owner and editor of the *Las Vegas Sun* newspaper described Hughes as "... a titan of unparalleled stature, who has given Las Vegas an image—a good image." He believed Hughes was good for Las Vegas and was opposed to any prying by his competition, *The Las Vegas Review-Journal*. In an editorial in the *Sun*, he wrote, "He (Hughes) remains a man who wants complete privacy; and local newsmen who pry into his affairs, and local newspapers who bandy his health and private life around on their front pages are doing the state of Nevada a great disservice."

Hughes was like the Wizard of Oz. Everyone knew of his great wisdom and power, but no one saw him. The secrecy that surrounded him led to remarkable stories and conjured tales, most of which were false. It was said he had died and a look-alike had taken his place. Some believed he was protected by hulking Cro-Magnons skilled in hand-to-hand combat who carried Thompson submachine guns. The truth was his so-called bodyguards were nothing more than mild mannered body servants who enjoyed the same mystique as their boss. Their power came from their access to Hughes, not from their physical prowess.

A reporter once remarked, "I wish I had X-ray vision. I would get a room on the top floor of the Frontier and look across the street through the walls of the Desert Inn to see if Hughes is really alive."

I chuckled when I read this statement because I had experienced dealing with a man who apparently had this gift while I worked a money laundering case. We were working an undercover operation on an attorney who claimed he could launder drug money through a bank on the island of Montserrat in the West Indies. I was standing in line waiting for my luggage to be screened by the X-ray machine when the machine broke down. A uniformed official took over and stood observing the exterior of the luggage as it passed by on a conveyor belt. As my briefcase passed, he stopped the belt and motioned me over. He ordered, "Open it!" My stress level began to skyrocket.

The briefcase contained two hundred and fifty thousand dollars in one hundred dollar bills. It was the Bureau's money. The inspector could easily have confiscated the money and arrested me, and the Bureau would never see the money again. I opened the satchel slowly, and the inspector's eyes got real big. Two undercover agents were in line behind me a few spots. The integrity of the investigation required that the undercover agents couldn't be connected to me. The agents acted quickly and moved to the plane. I pulled out my credentials and authoritatively announced, "This is official U.S. business." I then closed the briefcase, picked it up, and began walking to the plane waiting on the runway. I didn't dare turn around to see if I was being chased. I expected to hear "stop" and gunfire at any second. Fortunately, we boarded the plane and returned to the States successfully.

It was well-known in Las Vegas that bartenders, bellhops, and others "made arrangements" for customers to connect with prostitutes. Call girls, freelance hookers and even cocktail waitresses took advantage of the wide open market. Robert Maheu ran the Hughes casinos with an iron fist. Like most FBI agents, he wouldn't abide criminal activity. He was intent on pushing hookers out of his casinos. He ordered, "We will not tolerate any of our employees hustling women around here, and they know it."

At the time, Las Vegas law enforcement practiced cowboy justice. When it was learned a troop of Hell's Angels was headed for the city to party, the sheriff sent his deputies out to the Nevada-California line. They were armed with shotguns, and when the gang members arrived, they were stopped and ordered to "… go back where you came from." After a few tense minutes, the outlaws turned their bikes around and angrily went home. They realized they were outgunned.

Unfortunately, law enforcement's zeal to quell street crime didn't convert to stopping white-collar crime, corruption, or the taking of "black cash." This is a term often used by the mob to denote loot taken by stealth or larceny such as large scale skimming of cash from the count rooms of casinos. Maheu ran a clean place. He did what he could by cracking down on gambling cheats, employee theft, and various scams.

Hughes, like his father, prowled the vice lairs of Houston, Los Angeles, and Las Vegas. He had a voracious appetite for the flesh. Before his arrival at the Desert Inn, he used every hook conceivable to satisfy his cravings. As a young man, he and a girl-finder partner developed the technique of posing as talent scouts and convincing women that they should take a screen test. Many of the girls, yearning to be movie stars, complied with Hughes's every wish. Hughes, by nature, was very shy, so he used whatever trick available to capture his prey. He didn't view most women as individuals with feelings or dreams. He saw them as objects that performed various jobs or tasks important to him. This flaw in the man surely came from the example he had seen in his home as a child.

Later, when he became famous, the women were available for the picking. He voraciously sampled the movie stars of the day. Some say this included leading men as well. Looking into this piece of his world makes me feel like a peeping Tom peering in on an unseemly scene, but it was a part of the whole man that should be understood. It's been said, "There is no sense of time in Las Vegas—there are only shift changes." In his prime, Hughes stalked the city by night like a hungry predator. Show girls, movie stars, and in a pinch, prostitutes were his game.

Things had changed by 1967. An old friend of Hughes, a man who had been intimately involved in the womanizing days of Hughes's prime, visited him in his Las Vegas suite in early December 1967. He related, "I barely recognized the man. We had both grown older, but he looked very old. He was not the Howard Hughes that I knew." With drug addiction and serious mental aberrations weighing on his wearied shoulders, it isn't known how Hughes's libido faired during his descent into darkness.

• • •

Fate sometimes sets the stage for future events. I retired from the FBI in 1996. A short time later, a jewelry manufacturer, who was in Las Vegas for a jeweler's convention, hired me to guard a million dollars worth of jewelry. I baby-sat the valuables in the jeweler's Desert Inn suite while he schmoozed and entertained buyers. I became familiar with the interior of the Desert Inn as a result of this assignment. As I sat there for three nights, I had no idea that Howard Hughes had lived in the Desert Inn twenty-six years before, and I certainly didn't know that my knowledge of the interior would serve me later. The Desert Inn Hotel and Casino no longer exists. The two billion dollar Wynn Las Vegas resort now stands in its place on the famous Las Vegas Strip.

I had read some things about Hughes and his contested will and had heard about Melvin Dummar, but I had no personal knowledge of the facts. Although I had been stationed in the Las Vegas FBI field office since October of 1980, I had no occasion to search the investigative file nor talk to the agents who may have done some investigation into the case. When I arrived in Las Vegas in 1980, the case had been closed for over two years.

Between October 1967 and mid-1968, Hughes purchased the Castaways Casino for $3.3 million, and then he bought the Frontier Casino for $23 million. In mid-1968, he bought the Silver Slipper, Landmark, and Harold's Club for $33.2 million. He paid cash for all of them.

Hughes also bought a Las Vegas television station. He did this so that he could watch his favorite movies on TV, requiring them to be aired from midnight until four in the morning. Hughes also bought the 518-acre Spring Mountain Ranch west of Las Vegas. I've been to the ranch, and it's a lovely place. It sits nestled at the foot of the Spring Mountain Range. There are several natural springs on the property, and they provide water for crops and the lush vegetation that surrounds the very prominent ranch house.

The house was originally built by Gustav Krupp, a German steel and ammunition manufacturer who made a fortune supplying Nazi Germany during World War II. Hughes actually bought the property for Jean Peters, but she never came to see it. She had always wanted to live on a farm with animals and grass, and he had promised her that he would see to it that she had her dream one day. I suppose she was too devastated by his leaving her in California, and she never forgave him for that. She divorced Hughes in 1971, then remarried. She passed away in 2000.

Hughes spent every day confined to his bedroom. Even though his suite overlooked an incredibly beautiful golf course and pool, he never had the drapes open to see it. His staff occupied the rest of the floor. His personal aides occupied suites on the eighth floor. A sentry (a personal aide) was placed outside his door for the purpose of listening for his commands. Hughes often tapped a paper sack containing his discarded Kleenex tissues as a signal to the sentry. The Kleenex was an example of his obsession with germ contamination. He wiped everything clean with the ever present Kleenex.

It was Hughes's pattern to dive headfirst into new projects and then to turn the day-to-day operations over to his subordinates. He was notorious for turning out pages of handwritten memos and notes on yellow legal paper. The memos and the telephone were his conduit to the outside world. As time went on, Hughes, addicted to codeine and other drugs, became more and more removed from life. His many crashes had left him in pain, and the injected codeine gave him relief. He would slip in and out of lucidity, sometimes totally incapacitated, and at other times he was lucid and capable.

Hughes knew that he was deteriorating and didn't want to be seen in public. Extravagant steps were instituted to ensure that he was insulated. There were times when many in the public speculated that he was dead. Hughes's subordinates, particularly his closest aides, soon turned the tables on him by using his dependence on drugs as a tool to control him. In this way they took over much of Hughes's life. There were only a handful of aides who actually had face-to-face contact with him. At times, particularly near the end, this cabal essentially held Hughes prisoner in his own empire.

Robert Maheu was brought into Hughes's operations when Hughes moved to Las Vegas in 1966. Maheu, a former FBI agent and CIA operative, was viewed by Hughes as a man with connections who could get things done in Las Vegas, as well as nationally. Maheu, a grocer's son from

Maine, was paid half a million dollars a year for his services. Even though Maheu had never met Hughes face-to-face, they spoke daily on the telephone, often for hours at a time. Eventually Hughes became disenchanted with Maheu, and after a "civil war" within the ranks of Hughes's inner circle, Maheu was dismissed and left behind in the Las Vegas dust. Maheu had been accused of the unpardonable sin of trying to penetrate Hughes's inner circle by using one of the aides. Hughes believed that Maheu was trying to take over all of his operations, not just those that Maheu had been assigned. Hughes accused him of running an organization within the Hughes organization. Hughes was totally loyal to his inner circle, and they used this loyalty to destroy Maheu.

The personal aides, who were referred to by Maheu as zombies, took care of Hughes's daily needs. These people orchestrated a grand escape under the nose of Maheu and his men when Hughes was spirited out of Las Vegas on Thanksgiving Eve of 1970. There were two interior fire stairwells exiting from the ninth floor penthouse where Hughes lived. One went directly past the guard desk on the ninth floor, and the other exited on the other side of the penthouse. Hughes was carried down the hidden flight of stairs on a stretcher at 10:00 P.M. He was then whisked away to Nellis Air Force Base north of town, where a chartered plane was waiting to take him to the Bahamas. A second group of limousines was lined up in the parking garage. This decoy convoy left for McCarran International Airport. The entourage had carried out an immaculate escape plan for the purpose of eluding the guards on the ninth floor and sneaking out under the nose of Maheu.

Three years after escaping Las Vegas, Hughes gave a press conference over the telephone and was asked why he fired Maheu. He responded, "Because he was a no good, dishonest son of a bitch who stole me blind." Maheu brought a defamation lawsuit against Summa Corporation and won a $2.2 million dollar settlement for the defamatory statements made against him.

I interviewed Robert Maheu in Las Vegas. Maheu is a man who has been around the block a few times and has sophisticated street savvy. He said that he started working for Hughes in 1954, doing various jobs for him. In 1957, Hughes didn't want to appear before Congressional committees or hearings, so he engaged Maheu to take over those duties for him. Maheu stated that, "He wanted me to speak for him. I became his alter ego."

Maheu stated that when Hughes moved to Las Vegas, he called for Maheu to assist him there. As time went by, Maheu began gaining his trust, and the true powers within the Hughes organization began to worry about his relationship with Hughes. Maheu told me, "Bill Gay was trying to steal the Hughes Empire." And Gay had told Hughes, "Maheu was trying to take over your whole world."

In 1972, a federal investigation into Hughes's money dealings resulted in subpoenas being issued for various records. The Hughes organization reported that they couldn't comply because the headquarters office in California had been burglarized. Investigation by the police showed that someone had obtained the key to the front door, as well as the secret combination to a lock, and entered, undisturbed, and took documents. There were only six people within the Hughes's operation who had the combination. They all swore they hadn't shared it with anyone, but in the end, subpoenaed documents had vanished.

Learning details about Hughes and his lifestyle led me to

recall the various kings and emperors throughout history. Many were totally nuts. Others accomplished great things but had strange idiosyncrasies. Even some modern celebrities suffer from this flaw. Riches, combined with great power, do something to a man's ego. There's nothing he can't have at any time he wants it, or any way he wants it. It seems that Hughes's great wealth led him to a reality disconnect, and his eccentric tendencies forced him to live in his self-made world.

The fox was being chased by the hounds after he left the Desert Inn in November 1970. The IRS was hot on his trail. Hughes and his team fled to various destinations outside the United States. Hughes was degenerating at an increased pace by 1972. In December of that year, after leaving Managua, Nicaragua, because of an earthquake, Hughes's airplane landed in Miami, Florida. The IRS had a subpoena for Hughes relating to tax evasion. After overcoming the objections of Hughes's staff, the investigators entered the plane. The agents found a thin man with long, greasy hair and a beard. One agent stated, "He was emaciated, filthy, and unkempt, like a derelict. He could barely state his own name."

In an effort to avoid paying taxes, Hughes established the Howard Hughes Medical Institute and funneled funds into this tax exempt foundation. There were originally no employees, but after his death the tax hedge, now swimming in money, became a twelve billion dollar endowment to as many as 300 scientists conducting cellular and genetic research. The foundation spends $450 million a year on cutting edge science. Hughes used the institute to hide money, but the unintended consequence was that his money has been used for great good.

3

A Fantastic Story

Howard Hughes was besieged by personal demons throughout his life. In spite of this oppressive burden, he achieved the pinnacle of success. But fate can be a stern taskmaster, and his fall from grace was steady and ultimate. Hughes began a desperate journey in November of 1970. He left his luxury suite at the Las Vegas Desert Inn Hotel under the cover of darkness. He believed he had been betrayed by Bob Maheu, his chief of Las Vegas operations, and he was anxious to be rid of him.

Congressional committees were seeking to serve him with subpoenas, claiming possible misappropriation of government funds, and the scavengers of the IRS were tracking him. The Treasury Department was demanding millions of dollars in back taxes which Hughes refused to pay. He was a hunted animal. He and his entourage fled to the Bahamas in search of a sanctuary. Then, from the period of December

1970 through April 1976, this group of well funded vagabonds skipped from the Bahamas to London, to Vancouver, to Nicaragua, and finally to Acapulco, Mexico. Hughes was slipping into a dark hole, and by 1976 his deterioration accelerated. On March thirtieth of that year, it took him eight hours to drink a glass of milk.

"It was like a replay of a Keystone Cops movie. Everyone was in a panic. We were making phone calls trying to reach someone who would make a decision. The old man was sick. He was lapsing in and out of consciousness. He wouldn't eat. There he was, spread out like a cadaver, shriveled and lying flat on his back. It was a pitiful sight." This description was given by one of his aides as Howard Hughes neared his end.

Howard Hughes, the wealthiest man in America in 1976, a man of great accomplishment and power, was slipping away. There was no amount of money that could save him. Like all men, rich or poor, the mysterious enigma that was Howard Hughes was approaching the end that eventually comes to us all. He had built Hughes Tool Company, Hughes Aircraft, Hughes Electronics, and several airline companies into financial empires. As a young man, he had set several air speed records in an age of developing aviation. He had produced forty Hollywood movies. He was the most eligible bachelor of his time. He had been pictured on the covers of news magazines, and he had tried to buy up Las Vegas, owning as many as seven casinos and thousands of acres of land.

In Acapulco, one of the aides blurted out in desperation, "We've got to do something because it's going to look bad for us if the world finds out that he died looking like this."

Hughes had three physicians on his personal staff. One of them, Dr. Norman Crane, (now deceased) was asked after Hughes's death, "Why didn't you get your patient to a hospital in Acapulco, doctor?"

He answered, straight-faced, "Mr. Hughes didn't want to go to a hospital."

"Did you ask him?"

"No."

"Why not?"

"He was in a coma."

"Then how do you know he didn't want to go to a hospital?"

Crane stammered, "I – I – "

The attorney continued sarcastically, "You sensed this?"

He sheepishly answered, "Yes."

Another of Hughes's physicians inserted an intravenous line in the dying man's skeletal arm. He missed the vein, and the lower arm and wrist swelled up with intravenous fluid. His treated hand looked like a lobster claw. The inept doctors, realizing they could be in trouble, called for help on April 5, 1976. A Mexican physician responded immediately. He was disgusted with what he saw. He saw a man in the late stages of dying. His abdomen was swollen, a clear symptom of malnutrition. Hughes was a living skeleton. The doctor found no pulse rate or blood pressure, and told the aides if they would have gotten him to a hospital and put him on dialysis, they could have saved his life. Later, he said, "... it was apparent that the people around the patient were just waiting for him to die. He died of an illness called neglect."

The aides frantically reached out to another of the trio of personal physicians. He was on vacation in South America at the time, spending money provided by the dying man he was sworn to treat. Finally, after much cajoling, he reluctantly returned to Acapulco to assist the far spent Hughes. This delay erased Hughes's chances for survival. Critical time was wasted while waiting for the only practicing physician on the staff. This left Hughes in the care of inept, or worse, criminal conspirators. When the vacationing doctor arrived, they piled Hughes on board a plane and headed for Houston, Texas on April 5, 1976. Reservations were made for Hughes at Houston's Methodist Hospital using the alias, "J.T. Conner." Hughes was injected with medication in flight. It was thought to have been codeine, but no one would say for sure. Codeine is a pain suppressant. Hughes was in a coma and had no pain to suppress. At 1:27 P.M. no heartbeat could be found, and Hughes was declared dead.

Dr. Jack L. Titus (now deceased) chairman of the Department of Pathology at Baylor College of Medicine, performed an autopsy on Hughes on the following day. He found, "The eyes were still open. The pupils were thick and dilated. The time of death was around twelve noon, on the previous day. The body was of an elderly white male, about six feet three inches tall and weighed ninety-two pounds, emaciated—that is, thin with an implication of under-nourishment. The body was dehydrated, which means inadequate fluid." Titus stated that Hughes died of kidney disease, an ailment he had been affected with for at least ten years. After Hughes's death it was learned that Dr. Crane had been prescribing phenacetin for Hughes from 1946 through 1974. This drug is similar to aspirin, and prolonged use can lead to kidney failure. The doctors had also prescribed codeine for many years, and Hughes had become an addict.

At this point in time, Hughes's financial empire was bringing in $175,000 per hour, twenty-four hours a day. The autopsy also "... revealed chronic renal disease and signs of tertiary syphilitis. ... X-rays showed broken-off hypodermic syringes in Hughes's shriveled, needle-tracked arms." Drs. Forest Tennant (UCLA toxicology expert) and Jack Titus (Houston pathologist) both expressed their suspicions of a massive codeine overdose. Hughes had forty-five to fifty grams of codeine in his system as a result of a last injection. In 1969, Hughes was taking about two thousand three hundred dosage units of codeine per year. In 1975, he was taking five thousand five hundred units a year. This volume of dosage is only given to terminally ill patients. Titus also reported that Hughes's left shoulder had been separated from its socket two to three days prior to his death. No one could explain how this occurred.

Hughes was buried in Houston, Texas, in a velvet-lined copper and silver casket, on April 7, 1976. A red, white, and blue ribbon with the inscription, "He came. He saw. He conquered," draped the coffin. After many years of absence, he had finally come home. Twenty-five people attended the seventeen-minute funeral service. There were no tears shed. None of his aides or other employees were there.

The public outcry was furious. Various investigations were demanded. The Drug Enforcement Agency brought charges against Dr. Crane and John Holmes, a personal aide, and they were convicted of providing illegal drugs to Hughes. Another doctor was also charged, but was found not guilty. He made a financial settlement with the Hughes estate in a civil trial. No charges of homicide were brought, not even for negligent homicide, medical malpractice, conspiracy, or crime aboard an aircraft, despite the fact that an unconscious Hughes was injected with a heavy dose of what was believed to be codeine. The injection likely stopped his feeble heart.

After his death, the hunt was on for the Hughes will.

Approximately two weeks later, a mysterious will surfaced. The news broke like a shot in the silence.

"You won't believe it! They've found Howard Hughes's will, and Noah is the executor," exclaimed one of Noah Dietrich's close friends.

This exclamation started a rolling earthquake that resulted in the longest probate proceeding in American history. The events of the will's delivery and the probate trial were front-page stuff for months. It truly was a story stranger than fiction. The events fascinated the nation and led to the kind of media circus that wouldn't be seen again until the O.J. Simpson case, or the Michael Jackson frenzy.

On April 27, 1976, an information specialist for the Mormon Church found an envelope on the desk of his twenty-fifth floor office of the church office building. He had been away from his desk for a time and upon returning at 4:30 P.M., he had found a white, church visitor center envelope. The man had no idea where the envelope had come from. Written on the outside of the envelope was, "President Kimball."

The white quartzite Mormon Church office building was completed in 1972, in the historic center of Salt Lake City, Utah. The twenty-eight-story building is the nerve center for the twelve million-member worldwide church. The denomination's official name is The Church of Jesus Christ of Latter-day Saints, but the members are known as Mormons because of their belief in *The Book of Mormon*, which they consider a companion scripture to the *Bible*. The twenty-sixth floor of the building has a large observation deck that overlooks the city. The view is profound. It offers a panorama of the mighty Wasatch Mountains to the north and east, and the clean orderly, heavily treed streets of downtown Salt

Lake City. The office building's plaza is a peaceful place where people are encouraged to come and meditate. Benches and stone borders are placed throughout the large open area, and citizens and tourists often eat their lunches as they sit near the several fountains and enjoy the courtyard filled with gardens. The multicolored flowers, like so many painters' pallets, are abundantly placed in and around the area. Late April is the season of renewal for the city. The ornamental trees were in full bloom and the pink and white blossoms were bathed in the perfume of spring the day the will was surreptitiously delivered.

Why was an envelope addressed to the president of the church found on this low level employee's desk? It didn't make any sense. His job was answering letters addressed to the church. He only had fleeting contact with President Kimball. The concerned employee walked the envelope to President Kimball's personal secretary, and she delivered it to the head of the church. When he opened the envelope he found a note stating, "This was found by Joseph F. Smith's home in 1972. Thought you would be interested." There was another envelope inside addressed to "Dear Mr. McKay - Please see that this will is delivered after my death to Clark County Court House - Las Vagas [sic] Nevada – Howard Hughes."

In order to understand how the events fit together regarding the delivery of the will, it's important to know who was president of the Church of Jesus Christ of Latter-day Saints at the time of various events. David O. McKay served as president of the Mormon Church from 1951 through January 18, 1970, when he passed away. Joseph Fielding Smith served as president until he died on July 2, 1972. Spencer W. Kimball was installed as president on

December 30, 1973, and continued to serve until November 1985, when he passed away.

President Kimball called in the general counsel for the church on the following day. After a quick review of the various documents, including a three-page handwritten will on yellow lined paper, the lawyer said, "Here's a bequest for one-sixteenth to a home for orphans, and another to the Boy Scouts, and one-sixteenth to William R. Lommis [sic] of Houston, Texas, and one-sixteenth to Melvin DuMar [sic] of Gabbs, Nevada. Ever hear of either of them?"

President Kimball, a small man of great ability, had led the church to unprecedented growth to become a worldwide religion. He didn't respond to the question. He had no idea who the men were. He asked, "Surely, you aren't considering a possibility that this is genuine?"

The counsel pondered momentarily, "From the way it was left here yesterday, I'd say it has to be a forgery. But there are things about it that just don't look like a work of a forger."

The church often receives various hoax mail, communications from mentally troubled people and all kinds of solicitations. Kimball needed to know if there was a possibility the will was authentic. The next day, the church brought in a handwriting expert who was familiar with Hughes's handwriting. She reviewed the mystery will carefully. The church's lawyer watched in silence as she studied each page. After a time, he asked impatiently, "Was it written by Howard Hughes?"

She looked up from the pages, "It's possible to simulate a signature, but not three pages of writing."

The counsel asked, "Perhaps you might want to examine it further."

The expert didn't hesitate. "No. There's no need. I can

show you dozens of points of comparison, pen lifts, and line quality, and idiosyncrasies in the letter forms, even spacing. The man who wrote these pages and signed the name Howard Hughes was Howard Hughes."

Church officials questioned employees who may have had information about the will. One of those queried was a woman who sat at the information desk on the main floor of the church office building. She was a volunteer and enjoyed helping people. She greeted visitors, gave directions, and provided answers to questions. She was challenged by officials to search her memory about the events that had occurred one day before. She was stumped, but she recalled a tall woman, perhaps five foot eight, dressed in black, or possibly she had a black purse, or was it black hair? Her memory was sketchy. The woman was "well dressed and trim." She carried an envelope and asked where President Kimball's office was. The volunteer couldn't provide any other information of value, and couldn't say if the woman had, indeed, dropped off the will on the twenty-fifth floor.

Two days after receiving the will, Mormon Church officials flew to Las Vegas and turned the document over to the Clark County District Court on April 29, 1976. "How the envelope containing the papers was delivered to the headquarters of the church and who delivered it, we do not know," Wendell Ashton, the church's public-relations director, announced. "Circumstances surrounding delivery of the envelope frankly puzzled us after a day of extensive checking. Whether or not the will is the actual will of Mr. Hughes or is a hoax, we do not know."

The three-page handwritten will read as follows, errors in writing included:

Last Will and Testament

I, Howard R. Hughes, being of sound mind and disposing mind and memory, not acting under duress, fraud or the undue influence of any person whomever, and being a resident of Las Vegas, Nevada, declare that this is to be my last will and revolt [sic] all other Wills previously made by me -

After my death my estate is to be devided [sic] as follows -

first: one forth [sic] of all my assets to go to Hughes Medical Institute of Miami -

second: one eight [sic] of assets to be devided [sic] among the University of Texas - Rice Institute of Technology of Houston - the University of Nevada - and the University of Calif.

Howard R. Hughes

-page one-

Third: one sixteenth to Church of Jesus Christ of Latter-day Saints - David O. McKay - Pre.

Forth [sic]: one sixteenth to establish a home for Orphan Cildren [sic] -

Fifth: one sixteenth of assets to go to Boy Scouts of America.

Sixth: one sixteenth to be devided [sic] among Jean Peters of Los Angeles and Ella Rice of Houston -

seventh: one sixteenth of assets to William R. Lommis [sic] of Houston, Texas –

eighth: one sixteenth to go to Melvin DuMar [sic] of Gabbs, Nevada -

Howard R. Hughes

-page two-ninth: one sixteenth to be devided [sic] amoung [sic] my personal aids [sic] at the time of my death -

tenth; one sixteenth to be used as school scholarship fund for entire Country - the spruce goose is to be given to the City of Long Beach, Calif.

The remainder of my estate is to be devided [sic] among the key men of the company's [sic] I own at the time of my death.

I appoint Noah Dietrich as the executer [sic] of this Will -

signed the 19 [sic] day of March 1968

Howard R. Hughes

-page three-

Was this simplistic document the actual last will and testament of the richest man in America at the time? Hughes had been a major industrialist, aviation pioneer, movie producer, and he owned half of Las Vegas. He had lawyers waiting to secure his every wish. Surely he would have produced something more sophisticated than this shoddy product.

All sorts of wills began to surface after Hughes's death. The cockroaches came out from under their rocks to feed. There were approximately three dozen wills submitted to the courts in various jurisdictions. Some were obviously sincere efforts at fraud while others were sarcastically funny. One was from a woman in London who claimed she had shared a sandwich with Hughes in a park in 1949. Another left Hughes's estate to the "Richard Nixon School of Integrity and Honesty."

One joked, "... leave my hotels and casinos to the Boy Scouts so they can really have a good time." Another author, upset that the Mormon Church was named in the will wrote,

"Take the money from the Mormon Church and divide it among the Holy Baptist Church and Salvation Army." Another left Hughes's fortune to a topless dancer.

The handwritten will was so grossly prepared and of such poor quality that, if it were a forgery, it had to have been prepared by the dumbest, most inept forger in history. There was no effort to make it look legitimate. Or, on the other hand, a supremely cunning charlatan prepared it. Of course, a third option is that Hughes wrote it himself. In our society there is only one way to determine the answer to such a question. A trial would be held.

• • •

One of the beneficiaries named in the handwritten will was a "Melvin DuMar [sic] of Gabbs, Nevada." He was quickly identified as Melvin Dummar, formerly of Gabbs, Nevada. Who was this unlikely inheritor?

4

A Confession

The pre-trial proceedings were a sideshow. The media gorged itself on the tender meat of the events surrounding the will. The headlines shouted day in and day out, "Is the will a fraud?" "Dummar is the forger." "Experts say the Mormon will is legitimate."

Judge Keith C. Hayes (now deceased) was assigned to the case. He presided over Department Nine of the Clark County Court in Las Vegas, Nevada. Judge Hayes, a bookish man, had a reputation for integrity. He was soft spoken and believed in the concept that there is good in all men. At times, attorneys who appeared before him accused him of being naive. There were others who said he was fair and willing to give everyone a chance, but when a jury returned a verdict in a case, he had no difficulty in exacting hard penalties on those who were found guilty. He had sent several men to death row after their convictions for murder. His courtroom was found to be too small for the wildly popular proceedings, so the trial was moved to a larger courtroom to accommodate the press and interested spectators.

When Hughes died intestate (without a legal will), the longest and costliest estate battle in U.S. history ensued in the courts of Nevada. Because Hughes died without children, there were twenty-two heirs certified by a court in Texas. They were mostly maternal and paternal first cousins, who all fell in rank behind William Lummis and his mother Annette Gano Lummis, Hughes's aunt, who lived in Houston, Texas. When Hughes's parents died, he lived for a time with his aunt, Annette Lummis. When he left Houston for California, he gave his parents' home to her and her son William. Interestingly enough, William Lummis hadn't seen Hughes since they were children. When Hughes died, Lummis, an attorney, sued for legitimacy in a Las Vegas probate court.

Civil cases differ from criminal cases in many ways. In civil cases, sworn depositions are taken from potential witnesses before trial, and both sides are allowed to question the witnesses. The depositions are transcribed by a court reporter. At times, the deposition is read into the court record in place of the actual witness testimony. Because of these extensive depositions, the pretrial work is arduous and expensive. Many of the witnesses require the lawyers to travel out of state. In the meantime, investigative work goes on, legal research proceeds, and trial preparations continue in conjunction with the taking of depositions. All this requires a good team, and the delegation of duties is paramount. The team with the most money has the advantage. Money buys expert testimony, investigators, additional attorneys, and administrative help.

Trials can be fascinating studies in personalities, particularly those of the participating attorneys. There are overly confident, boisterous lawyers who stomp through the court-room like bison. There are frustrated thespians who think they are Shakespearian actors. And then there are buffoons, bluffing their way through the procedures. Of course, there are many dignified attorneys with clear, logical presenta-tions. Juries soon determine who is who.

Harold Rhoden was hired by Noah Dietrich (now deceased) to represent his interests as the named executor of the will. Rhoden was the lead attorney for the proponents of the will (arguing that the will was legitimate). He had been a World War II prisoner of war and a former Los Angeles Deputy City Attorney who was closely associated with Noah Dietrich. Rhoden quickly assembled a team of two attorneys besides himself. One of the attorneys was Marvin Mitchelson, famous divorce attorney to the stars. He spent money faster than he could earn it, and he saw a pot of gold at the end of the Hughes rainbow. Another was George Parnham, a young and inexperienced lawyer who has become a successful Texas criminal defense attorney. The team hired one investi-gator and a secretary. This proved to be insufficient. Rhoden, a small man with a Napoleon complex, wanted to run the whole show and found delegation of responsibility to be dif-ficult. The proponents were severely outgunned financially and were outnumbered by the contestants (those who fought the will's legitimacy).

When Noah Dietrich asked his attorney what the duties of an executor were, he was told, "Millions in fees! No, hun-dreds of millions! That's in ordinary fees alone!" The moti-vation for taking the case is very clear from this statement, but as time went on, Rhoden became a true believer as to the will's authenticity.

Jim Dilworth (now deceased), led the contestants.

Dilworth was a member of the same large and prestigious Houston Law Firm, that William Lummis, one of the heirs in the will, was a member of. Dilworth, a highly skilled litigator, lived behind the façade of a good ole boy. He was over six feet tall and weighed nearly three hundred pounds, and he played his image to the hilt. Many competent attorneys and investigators assisted him. He also had the extensive financial backing of his very successful law firm. He represented Annette Gano Lummis, (now deceased) in Dilworth's words, "The rightful heir and only surviving aunt of Howard Hughes."

The secondary counsel for the contestants was Paul Freeze (now deceased), a Los Angeles attorney hired by three of Howard Hughes's paternal cousins. A veteran of the Army, he graduated magna cum laude and was an experienced litigator. A third attorney for the contestants represented Terry Moore, a Hollywood B-movie actress who claimed to have married Hughes on board his yacht in 1947. A fourth team, hired by the Summa Corporation (Hughes' umbrella corporation) also contested the will. Chester Davis (now deceased), the hard-edged corporate counsel for Summa, hired a full investigative team.

Roger Dutson, an attorney from Ogden, Utah who had represented Melvin Dummar in the past, was on the proponent team, representing "Melvin DuMar {sic} of Gabbs, Nevada," a named inheritor. Dutson, realizing he needed assistance, formed a law firm of three, including himself, to represent the interests of Dummar. Dutson is currently serving as a judge in Utah. Dummar's attorneys took the case on a contingency basis. In order to earn a fee, they had to win, and if they won, they would receive a percentage of their client's benefits.

The contestants spent three million dollars on their investigation and the trial. The proponents were far behind financially. Rhoden received financial assistance from various friends including Mitchelson. Additionally, the universities and the Boy Scouts, with the exception of the University of Nevada, contributed forty thousand dollars to pay for daily transcripts. Melvin's lawyers contributed seventy-five thousand dollars for the European handwriting experts. Melvin chipped in what funds he could. The Church of Jesus Christ of Latter-day Saints took no official position on the will, but a wealthy member helped pay for daily trial transcripts. He agreed to be repaid after the trial, if they won.

The pretrial proceedings were contentious affairs. During the first pre-trial hearing, Judge Hayes, a man in his forties with a slight build and thinning brown hair, asked the attorneys to identify themselves for the record. Dilworth, ever the showman, his cowboy hat prominently placed on the table in front of him, stood and addressed the court. He was attired in a western style suit and wore alligator skin cowboy boots. He tried to steam roll over the court. "Jim Dilworth for the contestant William Lummis, your honor. It's our contention, your honor, that the three pages of this so-called will. . . ." He sputtered the words as if spitting a foul taste from his mouth. "Ah say these pages contain the filthiest forgery ever submitted to a court of the United States of America. The petition to have this garbage probated is an insult to the dignity of this most honorable court. It's a perpetration of a fraud, an' as lead counsel to mah client, Ah intend to do everything in mah power to bring the forger to justice. Your honor, never in mah twenty-five years as a trial lawyer in the great and sovereign state of Texas have Ah seen anythin' so rotten as—"

Judge Hayes interrupted, "Thank you Mr. Dilworth, but right now I'd like the record to reflect the appearance of counsel. Next."

The other lawyers introduced themselves. When Rhoden stood he requested that the Attorney General of Nevada conduct fingerprint and handwriting analyses of the will. Dilworth challenged the request, saying the fingerprint chemicals would destroy the writing on the will. Judge Hayes declined the request made by Rhoden.

The Nevada Attorney General's Office was appointed officer and friend of the court in the interest of the Nevada public and to give assistance to the court. The Attorney General's Office had argued that Hughes was the largest single employer in Nevada, affecting as many as twenty thousand to thirty thousand citizens. Thus, "the people" needed a representative.

At another hearing, Rhoden requested assistance from the Summa Corporation in locating Hughes's "body servants so we can subpoena them for depositions."

Dilworth took exception. He responded, "Ah take offense at the callin' of Mr. Hughes's executive staff assistants as 'body servants.' That's an insult to a fine group of loyal and dedicated executives!"

Rhoden retorted, "Whatever we call those middle-aged messengers, those mindless members of Howard Hughes's toilet paper platoon, Summa personnel know where they're hiding. And in trying to pry this information out of Summa, I've been paralyzed by their rigid policy of procrastination... These witnesses are all on the Summa payroll... They can give us the needed information."

Dilworth answered, "They're not hidin' out. They're on extended vacation."

The packed courtroom erupted in laughter. The judge pounded his gavel and ordered Summa to provide the information. John Holmes, one of the aides, refused to appear for the deposition, and a bench warrant was issued for his arrest. Freeze demanded that a warrant be issued for the arrest of Melvin Dummar for "artful deception."

The verbal fireworks continued. The lawyers were clearly playing to the crowd. The judge finally ordered the Nevada Attorney General to submit the will, the envelopes, and the note for fingerprint, handwriting, ink, and paper examinations by the FBI. They wanted a neutral investigation, so the documents were forwarded to the FBI laboratory in Washington, D.C.

My review of a Freedom of Information Request made by Brigham Young University revealed that an interesting debate had ensued within the Bureau about conducting FBI laboratory examinations on evidence in the Hughes probate trial. Conducting investigations in state civil matters is against FBI policy, as it would bog down the laboratory in the quicksand of countless civil trials. One side argued that the FBI had no jurisdiction. The other side argued that, technically, there was a potential federal crime in the use of interstate commerce in the delivery of the will, but more importantly, it was the high profile nature of the case that should be considered. The high profile argument won the day.

In the end, much of the case for the proponents hung on the testimony of Melvin Dummar. Dummar had admitted picking up an old, longhaired, disheveled man in the Nevada desert on or about December 29, 1967. The man had told him that he was Howard Hughes, but Dummar had continually denied ever seeing or handling the Mormon Will. When the FBI developed Dummar's left thumbprint on an envelope containing the will, his story crumbled. In an effort to produce the truth, Dummar was brought before Judge Hayes to be deposed in his courtroom. The press packed the seats, and a long line of spectators led from the courtroom, down the hall, into the lobby, and out to the street. On January 25, 1977, the whole world was watching as the high drama unfolded.

Dummar walked slowly to the witness stand. He appeared to be a man moving toward the execution chamber. Judge Hayes addressed the witness, "Mr. Dummar, under the Fifth Amendment of the United States Constitution, a person may refuse to answer any questions which may tend to incriminate him. Do you wish that protection?"

Dummar smiled sheepishly. "I don't see no reason to take the Fifth Amendment on anything."

"Then, anything you say here may be used against you in any criminal prosecution. Are you willing to testify?"

"Yes, sir."

"Mr. Rhoden, examine the witness."

Rhoden didn't know if Dummar would tell the truth or if he would concoct another wild tale. He showed Dummar a copy of the Mormon Church Visitor Center envelope and a note about Joseph F. Smith. "When did you write the words on the original of this envelope and this sheet of paper?"

"The day I left 'em in the church headquarters building."

"Where did you do the writing?"

"There."

"... You were asked in your deposition last month in Salt Lake City, if you had ever seen the visitor center envelope and the Joseph F. Smith note, and your answer was 'no.' You were lying, weren't you, Mr. Dummar?"

"Yes, sir."

"In the same deposition you testified that you had never seen the original of the purported will and its envelope. When you gave that answer, you were committing perjury, weren't you?"

"Yes, sir."

The sworn testimony continued for some time. "... While you're still on the witness stand, if you admit that you've been lying, your perjury may be wiped out. Is there anything in your testimony you would care to voluntarily change before you continue?"

"No, sir."

Dummar then went on to testify that a mystery man had delivered the will to his gas station in Willard, Utah. Rhoden then inquired, "Mr. Dummar, do you feel you have done something wrong?"

"Yes."

"What?"

"I lied to everybody about it. I lied to my lawyers. I lied to my wife. I lied to the reporters. I didn't tell the truth to nobody."

Dummar explained that he stayed with his story because, "The day after is when the news broke an' all the gravediggers started throwin' it at me, an' sayin' it was a forgery, an' I didn't wanna tell anyone I ever seen it or had anythin' to do with it."

Paul Freeze, a man who believed himself to be an extremely clever mouthpiece, questioned Dummar next. He wore a black, three-button suit, a white shirt, and a gray tie. His wing tip shoes were buffed to a shine. "... I understand that it's not uncommon for people to have trouble telling the truth—sick people called psychopaths. These unfortunate people have a disability given to them by God. I believe that in this area, you have a measure of admirable respect. Do you know what I'm talking about?"

"You mean, do I have respect for sick people who can't tell the truth?"

"No, respect for God."

"Oh, yes, I have respect for God."

Freeze went on to pound Dummar on his psychopathic and sociopathic tendencies. He must have expected Dummar to admit to being a sociopath even though one of the characteristics of sociopaths is their ability to lie without remorse. He accused Dummar of perpetrating a fraud on the court. After the bad cop charade, he played good cop. "... I will pledge to you that I would speak a whole day on your behalf to try to get you probation if you will now tell the truth. That is my pledge, and that is my deal."

Melvin responded simply. "I don't know whether that will is a forgery or not. I know I didn't forge it, if it is. That's all I've got to say."

The next day, it was time for the big Texan to take his turn. An indentation from his cowboy hat was evident on his hair as he stood. Dilworth tugged at his belt, then spouted, "You make me sick! Mr. Dummar, I have only a few questions for you." He went on to pummel Dummar with his previous testimony and lies for two hours. Finally he said, "Ah'm not gonna waste any more of my valuable time with you."

Witnesses can often be funny. I'll never forget a humorous occurrence during a trial of a mobster. One of the key witnesses was being pressed hard by the defense about his honesty. He responded, "I always tell the truth as far as I can stretch it."

In September of 1977, a pretrial hearing was held to

determine which side would have the burden of proof.
Rhoden was anxious to get on with his case and agreed to
have the burden of proof. This allowed Rhoden to make the
first opening statement and present his evidence first. It also
allowed him to make two summations. The burden of proof
means that the proponents were required to prove the
Mormon Will was written and signed by Howard Hughes by
the preponderance of the evidence. The contestants needed
only to show there was not a preponderance of evidence.

• • •

Willard, Utah, is a community of orchards and farms. Cattle
roam the thick grassland near Willard Bay, a large basin of
water fed by mountain streams. Fruit and vegetable stands
line the main road, and in season, they are stocked with
every imaginable type of fresh produce. It was April 27,
1976, and the buds on the fruit trees were beginning to
blossom. There had been no spring freeze, so the fruit har-
vest would be bountiful. There would be a bumper crop of
cherries, peaches, tomatoes, corn, melons, and pears.

The big rancher, strong and hardened by hours of labor,
was about to fill gas in his pickup truck at the Maverick station when a short, stocky man approached him. The stocky
man asked, "Is this Melvin Dummar's station? I have something important for him."

The rancher pointed down the road. He wasn't a man of
many words. "Down there, about quarter of a mile."

The stocky man got back in the passenger side of the car,
and the driver made a U-turn. They drove down the main
street until they came to the only other gas station in the
town of Willard. They pulled into the gas station, and the
stocky man went inside. He saw a man seated at a desk and
asked, "Are you Melvin Dummar?"

Dummar later testified about the encounter in the probate trial. He answered, "Yes, what can I do for you?"

The stocky man nodded his head. "Did you hear about Howard Hughes dying?"

Melvin looked quizzically at the stranger. He wanted to tell the man what a stupid question that was, but instead he responded, "Yeah, everybody has heard about it. It's big news."

The man smiled slightly. "Wouldn't it be something if you were in his will and got some money from the Hughes estate?"

The repressed memory of December twenty-ninth, nine years before, flooded Melvin's mind. He wondered, could there be some connection between this short stocky man and the cold December night in 1967 when he had rescued an old vagrant in the Nevada desert?

"Yeah, it sure would!" Melvin responded.

A customer pulled up to the gas pumps and, since it was in the days of full service, Melvin went out to wait on the customer. A short time later he returned to the office and found the stranger gone. He was mystified as to what the man's conversation was leading to. As he sat down at his desk, he noticed a white envelope on top of some papers he had been working on. He hadn't noticed it before. Written on the envelope was, "Dear Mr. McKay, please see that this will is delivered to the Clark County Courthouse in Las Vagas [sic] after my death. Howard Hughes."

Melvin had all but forgotten his experience with the old man in the desert. He and Bonnie, his second wife, lived on the second floor of a red brick building, and they both operated the Chevron service station on the first floor. Melvin was attending Weber State College as a part-time night school student. He was taking various real estate courses at the time as he was struggling financially with the gas station. This was because business had dropped off by more than half when Interstate 15 was completed, thereby bypassing Willard.

Melvin was mystified. "Curiosity was driving me crazy. I wanted to know what was in the envelope." He stared at the envelope for some time, turning it over in his hands. In doing so, he noticed a red Pitney Bowes imprint across the back seal of the envelope. Melvin made a decision. He'd open the envelope and learn what was hidden inside. Melvin is a man of impulse. His emotions often drive him to improvident action. He rationalized that whatever was in the envelope must be important. After all, the stranger had taken the trouble to hand deliver it to him. There was nothing sacrosanct about the envelope. It was addressed to "Mr. McKay." Melvin assumed this was David O. McKay, former president of the Mormon Church. He was long deceased, and the envelope had been delivered to Melvin, so he assumed he should know what it contained. Most reasonable people would probably do the same.

Using the technique he had developed while opening his ex-wife's mail without leaving a trace, he confessed, "I steamed it open. I took an electric frying pan and filled it with water. When it began to steam, I held the envelope over the rising steam. There were spots that remained glued so I put the envelope in a toaster oven to melt the remaining glue. This process scorched the edges of the envelope. It finally opened. I took out three yellow handwritten pages from the envelope and read them. At the bottom of each page was the signature, 'Howard Hughes.' After reading the will, I panicked. I was named in the will. It didn't make any sense. This was way too big for me. This must be a joke. Why bring this to me?" Melvin stressed, "It totally scared the living hell out of me. If it was real, I had to do something with it. I didn't know what to do. I didn't think of the police or attorneys. It never crossed my mind. The way the will was addressed, I thought, well, maybe I should take this to the church." Melvin then reglued the envelope.

Melvin had read the will several times. He wondered if it could possibly be a legitimate document. If it was, then finally, fate had smiled on him. He stood to inherit some-where in the neighborhood of one hundred and fifty million dollars, one-sixteenth of Hughes's vast estate, according to experts. Adding for inflation, Melvin's share today would be nearly half a billion dollars. After all the years of financial struggling, and holding back the story about picking up a man who identified himself as Hughes for fear of being called a fool, now maybe he had struck it rich. Melvin for-got that fate can be a fickle mistress. She can kiss you and entice you, but then without warning, she can slip away.

When the news broke that the Hughes will had inexpli-cably been dropped off at the Mormon Church Headquarters, it was immediately named the "Mormon Will" by the media. The news rolled across the nation in newspapers and on television. When copies of the will were made public, Melvin became an overnight celebrity. His phone started ringing, and at first, he had fun as the nation's newest celebrity. He told his story about picking up an old man somewhere between Beatty and Goldfield, Nevada, many times. He explained that he didn't know if the man was Howard Hughes or not, but he had told Melvin he was. Eventually the pressure became overwhelming. The feeding frenzy was on. Melvin appeared on every national morning news program and was treated like a king. He related his story over and over again, but he never admitted to seeing the will or receiving it. Later, in 1980, an Academy Award-winning movie entitled, *"Melvin and Howard"* was made. It enjoyed some success, but according to Melvin, it portrayed the events using substantial literary license. He says he didn't make any money from the movie.

Although Melvin was a member of the Church of Jesus Christ of Latter-day Saints, he had not been active or involved for many years. His life had led him elsewhere. He knew where the church headquarters in Salt Lake City was, and he knew that David O. McKay was no longer the president of the church. He didn't say anything to his wife because he didn't want to cause a huge commotion, so he asked her to handle the station, as he had to run an errand.

Melvin drove to Salt Lake City, about an hour south of Willard, not knowing where President Kimball's (the president of the Mormon Church at the time) office was located. He said he first went to the visitor's center inside Temple Square. Temple Square is a walled, square block in the historic heart of the city. It houses the Mormon Temple, the Tabernacle, and several other historic buildings.

The Mormons were driven out of Illinois in the winter of 1846 after a mob murdered their leader and prophet, Joseph Smith. They fled across the Mississippi River and battled the elements at a place called Winter Quarters, where many died from the cold and other privations. In an unparalleled modern exodus led by colonizer Brigham Young, they traveled across one thousand miles of the American frontier in wagons and handcarts looking for religious freedom, a promise guaranteed by the Constitution, but denied to them by men. On July 24, 1847, after one hundred and eleven days, the lead elements of the wagon train came to a summit over-looking the Great Salt Lake Basin, and Brigham Young was heard to say, "This is the place." Utah, the second driest state in the nation, became the forty-fifth state to join the Union. In 2004, one hundred and fifty-seven years later, the Illinois legislature passed a resolution apologizing for the brutal actions taken against the Mormons in Illinois.

Utah derives its name from the Indian tribe known as the Utes. They called themselves "Nucia," their word for "The People." These hunter-gatherers roamed the grasslands and mountains seeking game, nuts, seeds, berries, and roots to sustain them. They had acquired horses from the Spanish explorers as early as 1680. The famed Spanish Trail cut through parts of Utah on its way to California. The topography of the state is varied. It rises from the salt-encrusted flats around the Great Salt Lake, the largest natural lake west of the Great Lakes. Its twenty-seven percent salt far exceeds the salt content of the ocean. The sagebrush and grasslands spread across the state and advance into the foothills covered with pinion pine, juniper, and cedar trees. The Rocky Mountains run the length of the state and are blanketed with varied conifers and aspen groves. In the South the landscape changes dramatically. The vermilion cliffs of Zion National Park, the goblin formations of Bryce Canyon National Park, and the stone natural bridges of Arches National Park provide unique scenic spectacles. The pioneers began settling Salt Lake Valley, which was barren and uninhabited by the Indians. The settlers refined the ancient practice of irrigation, and the precious water from several canyon streams was diverted to the farm fields. They built a temple and a tabernacle. The construction of their holy temple took forty years. The six spires of this granite edifice reach to the sky and is a majestic testament to their faith.

The eight thousand-seat Mormon Tabernacle is an architectural marvel constructed by a pioneer bridge builder. The spans of the roof are bound together with rawhide straps and wooden dowels. The tabernacle is home to the world famous Mormon Tabernacle Choir.

The history of Utah is essentially a history of Mormon colonization. Brigham Young sent settlers to the corners of the state. They were people seeking to find a place of protection and safety where they could live in peace and grow their crops. By 1860, there were forty thousand people in the state. Most were Mormon converts from the East, South, and Midwest. Thousands of others were from northern Europe and England. They were rugged people who challenged a rugged land.

At the Mormon Church Visitor's Center, Melvin asked if he could speak to President Kimball. He was told the president's office was on the twenty-fifth floor of the Church Office Building across the street. On his way out, Melvin picked up a visitor's center envelope and a sheet of paper. He hurriedly scrawled on the paper, "This was found by Joseph F. Smith's house in 1972. Thought you would be interested."

Melvin testified in a sworn affidavit about receiving the will, "... I can remember him telling me something about a will of Howard Hughes being found in Salt Lake City... I think he said it was found somewhere around Joseph Smith's house. I can't remember exactly... He told me it was in 1972." He thought the mystery man who delivered the will to him in Willard may have mentioned it.

Melvin wrote "President Kimball" on the new envelope, placed the old envelope containing the will in the new envelope along with his note, and walked across the street.

Melvin told me that he had added the Joseph F. Smith information to explain how he got the will. He didn't want to mention the mysterious, short, stocky man because he had no idea who he was or where he had come from. He couldn't recall why he chose the name of Joseph F. Smith. He was sure that someone had told him to say he had gotten the envelope at Joseph F. Smith's home. He explained that since Hughes died on April 5, 1976, many people came into Melvin's gas station and mentioned Hughes's death. It was big news in the little community of Willard. Hughes was somewhat of a folk hero in the area because he employed so many Mormons on his personal staff.

Melvin is certain that one of these visitors, just prior to the delivery of the will, told him about Joseph F. Smith and about something being found at his home. Melvin has searched the recesses of his mind, but twenty-nine years have erased the details of this memory. He explained that when the will came to him, he associated it with coming from the home of Joseph F. Smith and wrote that information on the slip of paper that he enclosed in the envelope that was delivered to the Mormon Church.

At this point, I had the sense he was holding something back. He adamantly denied it, but a piece was missing, and I thought he was holding that piece.

Melvin took the elevator to the twenty-fifth floor of the church office building and spoke to a receptionist behind a desk. He asked to see President Kimball, but he was told that he couldn't see him without a proper appointment. Now he didn't know what to do. He walked down the hall, his mind racing. As he approached the elevator, he noticed an empty desk with some papers on it. As impetuous as ever, he walked into the office and laid the envelope on the desk and then hurried out. He thought that he had done his part and that the church would handle the will. His responsibility was completed. A weight had been lifted from his shoulders. All he had to do was wait for events to unfold.

The newspapers reported that a woman who worked for the church was interviewed by a reporter, and she said the will may have been delivered by a tall, trim woman. Melvin took this news as a good cover for himself. He thought no one would ever know that the will had been in his possession and that he had delivered it to the church. He believed he was totally out of the picture. This decision was a major mistake on his part and would come back to haunt him during the probate trial. He swore to me that he hadn't dressed like a woman when delivering the will. He's probably telling the truth as he certainly couldn't be described as "trim."

After the will came to light, Melvin received calls from all kinds of people. They wanted money, and one person even threatened him, saying he'd better tell everyone that he had been with Melvin when he picked up Hughes. He and his wife finally hid from the press by taking refuge in a friend's house. Melvin was having difficulty maintaining his sanity. On one television network he exclaimed, "I wish to God this never happened. It's a terrible nightmare." He had never been good under pressure, and he felt his mental stability cracking.

Melvin had sown a poison seed in telling his story time and again. He had denied knowing anything about the will. He told about the rescue of Hughes, and said he hadn't known about the will until he read about it in the newspaper because, "I was afraid that if I told them the truth, they would think I had something to do with writing it, and they would call it a fraud and call me a crook." He said he regrets the lie to this day.

Melvin stuck to his story about knowing nothing about the actual will until disaster struck. It hit him like a hammer. The FBI developed a latent fingerprint of Melvin's left thumb on the visitor center envelope that had been delivered to the Mormon Church. Now the pressure was on. Melvin was exasperated.

"I was hammered until I almost had a nervous breakdown," he confessed.

Later, when confronted by his attorney during preparation for the probate trial, Melvin became emotional and began to sob. The pressure was crushing him. After receiving a brow-beating by his attorney, Melvin finally came clean and told about the delivery of the will at his gas station. This is when he was required to give a sworn deposition in Judge Hayes's courtroom. Melvin went on to testify unwaveringly in the trial as he recounted the story of the will.

The stocky phantom, who Melvin said delivered the will to him, turned out to be LeVane Malvison Forsythe (now deceased), a noble name for a shady character. He has been described as a fireplug. He was a contractor who had originally lived in California, but had subsequently moved to Alaska. He told a story as remarkable as Melvin's.

LeVane Forsythe, a burly construction worker who talked like a drunken sailor, first met Hughes on a movie set in Ventura, California, in 1946 or 1947. Forsythe had observed members of the film crew stealing from the set when Hughes was away. He took the opportunity of confiding this information to Hughes, and Hughes expressed his gratitude. Hughes was a man who moved instinctively, and he approached Forsythe to become his confidential agent for special projects. The offer of pay was good, so Forsythe agreed. Hughes gave him the code name "Ventura" so that

Forsythe would know it was a Hughes representative calling. Over the years, Ventura performed many jobs for Hughes. Most of the jobs consisted of delivering envelopes to various people, including politicians. He refused to identify the politicians. Forsythe explained that many of the envelopes contained large sums of cash.

He stated that he had been summoned by Hughes to meet him at the Bayshore Inn in Vancouver, British Columbia, during the latter part of July or early part of August 1972. Hughes's aides denied the meeting, but the aides destroyed the daily logs of Hughes's activities before leaving Canada. Were they trying to cover up the meeting, or were they just housecleaning?

Forsythe said he met Hughes, who was alone, and Hughes "… told me why I was there, why he had requested me there—that he had a brown envelope that was laying on the table and he wanted me—to entrust me with it. And that I was, I would probably be retaining it for some time—And wanted to know if I would accept that responsibility, and that the document, the brown envelope, contained instructions in case of his death. And he asked me if I was willing to accept that responsibility… I told him I would accept that responsibility."

Hughes resided in the Bayshore Inn in Vancouver, B.C., from March 1972 through most of August of that year. According to Forsythe, Hughes told him "… somebody else had held the will but they didn't want the responsibility to hold it anymore."

The probate court records show that sometime in July, probably before Forsythe's meeting with Hughes, an anonymous man called a judge in Salt Lake City. The judge testified that the caller told him he had a packet with an envelope addressed to Mr. McKay. He told the judge that he had acquired the packet containing Howard Hughes's will near the home of Joseph F. Smith in Salt Lake City.

Joseph Fielding Smith, president of the Mormon Church, had sadly passed away on July 2, 1972. The man said the will was to be filed upon Howard Hughes's death. The man asked what he should do, as Mr. McKay was dead. The judge told the caller to hold it until Hughes passed away, then to follow the instructions in filing it.

Who was the previous caretaker of the will? It might have been one of Hughes's aides or another Hughes secret operative. The caretaker didn't get any assistance from the judge, so he returned the will to Hughes. His testimony could have corroborated a portion of Forsythe's testimony. Why didn't this man come forward during the trial?

Hughes told Forsythe not to open the envelope until he had passed away. Forsythe kept the envelope for approximately four years, and when he learned Hughes was dead, he opened the package. Inside, he found three individual envelopes: one for Chester Davis, Hughes's corporate attorney, one for Mr. McKay, and one with two thousand eight hundred dollars in one hundred dollar bills for himself. Forsythe testified that on January 7, 1976, three months before Hughes died, he received a telephone call from an unidentified male who used the code name Ventura. Forsythe was instructed to deliver the will in the envelope to Melvin Dummar in Willard, Utah, in the event of Hughes's death. Forsythe said he had no idea who the caller was.

Chester Davis provided a sworn deposition for the trial, but inexplicably, was never asked about the envelope that was reportedly mailed to him by Forsythe. His answer to the question would have been extremely enlightening.

Forsythe came forward in February of 1977, because, as

he testified in a deposition, he had received a phone call from a man identifying himself as Dan Harper. Harper said, "What's Ventura? I figured it out, and I think you were the one who dropped off the will to that kid in Utah. The will is in trouble in Las Vegas because the kid you left it with said he had never seen it, and they caught him lying." The caller said that he had found Forsythe's name in Hughes's papers. He didn't know who Forsythe was, but he had determined that he was Ventura. The caller gave the name and phone number of Melvin's attorney to Forsythe. Forsythe was told he needed to testify, as Melvin had screwed everything up by lying. Forsythe was reluctant and fought the idea. He finally relented and told his story about the will in a deposition.

I couldn't find any evidence of a Dan Harper being employed by Hughes. This must have been a fictitious name used by the caller to cover his true identity. I wondered, why didn't this person come forward during the trial? Could he have been the same person who had held the will prior to Forsythe?

Forsythe admitted to flying to Salt Lake City on April 26 or 27, 1976, after Hughes's death. He hired a car and a driver and found his way to Willard, Utah, where he asked someone where Dummar's gas station was, then he delivered the will to Melvin. He later testified he couldn't understand why he was delivering the will to Dummar because, "... it didn't make no sense to me... Where I was at didn't make no sense. Delivering something of this nature to this—this person—didn't make no sense to me. Why would Hughes want instructions about his death or will to be delivered to this kid in this gas station?"

He said that he had engaged Melvin in some small talk and had asked what Melvin would think about inheriting money from Hughes. He then left the envelope on Melvin's desk as Melvin was waiting on a customer.

Forsythe swore that when he opened the large envelope given to him by Hughes, he found three smaller envelopes inside. One was labeled "deliver this." This was the will envelope. One was labeled, "Chester Davis." He mailed this to Davis. And one envelope was labeled, "open this one." This envelope contained two thousand eight hundred dollars in one hundred dollar bills, which he testified he deposited the day Hughes died.

Before Forsythe provided his deposition, he was administered a polygraph examination by Dr. David Raskin, Ph.D., a professor at the University of Utah. The following three questions were asked:

> In Vancouver, in 1972, were you given an envelope by Howard Hughes?

> On or about January 7, 1976, did you receive telephone instructions to deliver to Melvin Dummar one of the smaller envelopes contained in a large one given to you by Howard Hughes?

> Did you deliver the envelope to Melvin Dummar in Utah on April 27, 1976?

Forsythe answered "yes" to each question, and Dr. Raskin reported that Forsythe had scored a fourteen in his responses and that a ten is considered a "... totally reliable indication of a subject's truthfulness." He believed Forsythe was telling the truth.

A polygraph is sometimes called a lie detector, but in

reality it detects changes in physiological responses. It measures respiration (breathing rate), heart rate, blood pressure, and galvanic skin response (sweat). The polygraph measures these involuntary reactions to key questions and records them on a sheet of graph paper. It's very difficult to beat the machine if a qualified examiner administers it. A sociopathic personality can beat it, only because the sociopath has no remorse or sense of right or wrong and can lie without hesitation. The average citizen's body reacts involuntarily to the questions and usually gives a correct reading. Polygraphs are not usually admissible in court, but they certainly are a strong indicator of investigative direction.

Forsythe corroborated Melvin's story about the delivery of the will. Did this mean that they were telling the truth, or were they in collusion in a grand scheme to pull off the scam of the century? Also, during the trial, the opponents with all their resources, were never able to make any connection between Melvin and Forsythe outside of the will delivery. They pulled out all the stops on that portion of their investigation but found nothing.

The standard of proof that weighs the evidence in criminal cases is "proof beyond a reasonable doubt," but as this matter is a civil case, I'll use the lesser standard of "preponderance of evidence." This means the evidence must have superior importance, weight, force, or quantity. The evidence must be dominant one way or the other to have a successful verdict.

This case was starting to get interesting. I decided the challenge of finding the truth would be a daunting one. It would take all my experience as an investigator and could lead in many directions.

5

The Trial

I needed to know what happened during the trial. What evidence was presented? Was there anything that was out of the ordinary? Why did the jury rule the way it did? I would have to plow through volumes of documents to find the answers. In time, I would also need to speak with those who were present at the trial to get details not found in the written record.

Candidly, trials aren't necessarily a search for the truth. Justice is usually achieved, but the proceedings often evolve into legal and intellectual combat between the adversaries. The trial often becomes a contest, like a tennis match, each side looking for the win. Criminal trials differ from civil trials in many ways. For example, no one is ever found innocent in a criminal proceeding. The jury either finds the defendant guilty or not guilty. If found not guilty there has to be reasonable doubt of guilt. This doesn't necessarily mean the defendant is innocent. It means that there wasn't enough evidence to convict beyond a reasonable doubt. I've testified in too many criminal trials and hearings to remember them all, and I've sat at the prosecutor's table for days on end, as is the practice for case agents in federal court. Trials are usually tedious and seldom exciting. This is especially true in many civil trials. John sues Bob for money owed. Betty sues the insurance company for a slip and fall. It can be painfully tedious stuff.

The cases are laid out a block at a time, and the blocks are stacked until a picture becomes clear. The opposition essentially tries to tear down as many blocks as possible so that the picture is no longer so clear. This is the adversarial system that has served us for many years in this country. There are few startling revelations that blow a case wide open in real life because both sides, for the most part, know what the evidence is before the trial begins.

Power in society emanates from rank, wealth, or strength. Trials are a means to level the playing field, to equalize the power. But to think that justice is served in each trial is a fool's fantasy.

The Hughes probate trial began on November 7, 1977. It took two weeks to pick a jury. Each side had four peremptory challenges. They could dismiss any four people from the jury pool for no explained reason. After everything was said and done, the probate jury consisted of three women and five men. By this time, Rhoden owed Mitchelson eighty thousand dollars, and two other people sixty-five thousand dollars. He sold his airplane and took out a second and third mortgage on his home for one hundred thousand dollars. A Houston court was simultaneously convened to determine Hughes heirs should the Mormon Will be found illegitimate. The trial ran for eight months. The testimony was voluminous, and at times it was stupefying. In the interest of sanity, I have tried to pare down the most pertinent material. Hopefully, the flavor of the evidence will be understood.

Because the proponents had the burden of proof, they were given first opportunity to make an opening statement. The diminutive Rhoden stood at the attorney's podium and began his case presentation. He turned and smiled at the jury, then proceeded, "Members of the jury, you'll find that LeVane Forsythe is a crude bagman, sophisticated in the ways of the gutter. A believable witness? No! He'll testify that he received the will from Howard Hughes and was later instructed to deliver it to Melvin Dummar. A believable story? No! No, not until you hear the testimony of witnesses whose credibility you can't question, and see evidence on paper that will compel you to believe Forsythe..."

Rhoden felt confident. He had a good case, and like all good trial lawyers, he loved being in the spotlight. He continued, "You'll find that Melvin Dummar is a gentle dunce. He committed perjury when he denied that it was he who had delivered the will to the Mormon Church headquarters in Salt Lake City. Dummar will tell you that on April 27, 1976, a stranger dropped the will off at Dummar's gas station. An unbelievable story told by an unbelievable witness. Unbelievable, until you hear and see evidence that proves he's telling the truth—evidence such as the testimony of agents in the scientific labs of the FBI."

He smiled slyly, then continued. "The will itself is bizarre. Bizarre in what it says, in the way it was written, and in the way it was held for eight years. And bizarre in the way it was delivered to the Mormon Church. But this could have been another example of the bizarre ways of the man who wrote it."

Rhoden felt he had the jury's rapt attention. He went on, "... after Noah Dietrich left Hughes in 1957, Hughes slid into a deep pit of seclusion, surrounded by worms who were his personal aides. From the testimony of these aides, and others from whom he bought obedience, and from his hand-written memos, you'll piece together a true picture of Howard Hughes. Not a brave pilot. Not the inventive aero-nautical genius. Not the decisive industrialist. That's the legend, but not the truth... (Hughes) was a spoiled boy who had grown old but not up... In 1966, Howard Hughes moved with his attendants onto the entire ninth floor of the Desert Inn Hotel here in Las Vegas... Members of the jury, from your own examination of the will in comparison with hundreds of samples of Hughes's handwriting, you will see that the offered will was written by Howard Hughes."

Now it was the contestants' turn to make opening statements. Freeze stood up stiffly. Freeze straightened his tie, then plunged into a litany of promises. He promised that the will was a fraud. He promised that he would prove that Bonnie Dummar, Melvin's wife, had forged the document in a conspiracy with her husband. He also promised to prove that Dummar and Forsythe were in collusion in the delivery of the will. He droned on, but he essentially made promises that he would prove wrongdoing with regard to the will.

Dilworth was ready to go the moment Freeze sat down. He got to his feet slowly. He pulled on his belt as if preparing for a fistfight. He walked slowly to the center of the courtroom, near the podium. He wasn't going to be hobbled by some arbitrarily placed piece of furniture. He sauntered up to the jury box, and smiled graciously at his attentive audience as he tucked his huge hands in his pants pockets. "Ladies and gentlemen of the jury. Ah know y'all are getting tired of hearin' lawyers talk to you, so Ah'll be brief. Ah'd jest like to kinda visit with y'all for a few minutes to simplify this case. Ah know you're gunna let your minds be poisoned by Mr. Rhoden's openin' remarks, like callin' Mr. Hughes's executive staff assistants—those fine, God-fearin' men—callin' them worms… For example, here's one fact. In Salt Lake City, Utah, last December, when we took the deposition of Melvin Dummar, we let him know that we found his fingerprints on the Mormon Church Visitor's Center envelope. That's the envelope he put his forged will into when he delivered it. An' at lunch that same day, Mr. Rhoden told Melvin Dummar that if we did have his fingerprints on that envelope, Dummar could safely lie and state that someone had planted them there."

Rhoden objected strenuously.

Dilworth gave an "oh, gosh" smile, then retreated. "All right, all right, all right. Ah'll withdraw mah remark an' the jurors can disregard it. Now, ladies and gentlemen, let me show you how simple all this really is. This so-called will names Melvin Dummar as a beneficiary. Melvin claims that Mr. Hughes knew him because one fine night in late December 1967, Melvin Dummar, the good Samaritan, picked up Howard Hughes in the Nevada desert an' gave him a lift to Las Vegas. An' a quarter. But we're gonna show you that Howard Hughes didn't leave the Desert Inn at any time in December 1967. In fact, he didn't leave it once in the four years he was there. Therefore, Howard Hughes could not have met Melvin Dummar in the desert. An' therefore, Howard Hughes could not have written a will namin' Melvin Dummar. An', therefore, this is a forgery!"

Melvin was the star witness for the proponents. He testified in the trial and stuck to his story about the delivery of the will and his trip to the Mormon Church headquarters. He also testified about picking up an old man in the Nevada desert in late December 1967. He testified that the old man told him he was Howard Hughes. This testimony was corroborated by his ex father-in-law and Linda Diego, his ex-wife, and others that he had told about picking up Hughes in early 1968. They said he had mentioned picking up a man who identified himself as Hughes.

In an effort to cast doubt on his truthfulness, Melvin was cross-examined intensely and his arrest record was exposed. Much was made of the fact that he had participated in several television game shows such as "Let's Make a Deal," where participants were required to wear costumes and that on one occasion he used the name of his father-in-law when he won a car. Attorney Freeze tried to emphasize this was done to show Melvin's predisposition to playing roles and scamming others. Freeze, a perfectly descriptive name for him, wouldn't let up on this line of questioning. He pummeled Melvin for several hours until the judge stepped in and stopped the agony.

After Melvin's testimony, his co-conspirator, according to Freeze, took the stand. Bonnie Dummar, Melvin's wife since 1973, testified in the trial. She was asked if Melvin had ever told her about picking up Hughes. She responded, "I don't think Mel ever told me that until the will was found."

The questioning continued by Rhoden. "When did you first learn that it was your husband that delivered that will to Mormon Church headquarters on the twenty-seventh of April, 1976?"

"It was in January of 1977, the night Mel admitted it to me."

"What did you say to him when he told you that he had delivered it to the Church?"

"I said, 'You're kiddin'.' An' that was the night he asked me if I had anything to do with it. I couldn't believe he actually suspected me."

"Now, Mrs. Dummar did you commit the crime (forgery of the will) that Mr. Freeze accused you of committing?"

"Of course not!"

Cross-examination consisted of submitting into evidence Bonnie Dummar's handwriting, including the misspellings of some of the same words misspelled in the will. Bonnie described herself as a fair speller, even though she only completed the ninth grade. Also, the fact that she had spent time in jail on a charge of making a false statement was brought up. She was later asked by Rhoden, "Mrs. Dummar, you want to explain this matter of your welfare fraud conviction? Explain it."

"Well, my first husband left me several times. He'd leave me every time I was pregnant, an' I had to go on welfare 'cause I couldn't work, an' he didn't support me. He'd leave an' keep comin' back an' then leave again, an' come back, an never give me any money except for car payments an' for extra food for him. So one day I called the welfare people an' told 'em about this, an' the next thing I knew they put me in jail."

Forsythe's deposition was read into the record by Rhoden. In it he told his story about being given a secret mission by Hughes to hold the will until his death. He also testified that he had delivered the will to Melvin in Willard, Utah.

On cross-examination during his deposition, Forsythe was asked about criminal charges of embezzlement and forgery brought against him in Torrance, California.

Forsythe responded by explaining, "After I dumped

them crooks outta there, they got together an' accused me of embezzlement. I didn't embezzle nothin'. Two of them people who made the phony charges against me was a coupla lunatics. This was the Southwestern Association of Retarded Children, an' some of the people involved in it made them kids look…"

"What were you charged with, Mr. Forsythe?"

"The jury found me not guilty."

There was also a discrepancy in flight schedules between Anchorage, where he lived at the time, and Salt Lake City. Forsythe had inexplicably added flight information, after the fact, to his appointment calendar in order to bolster his deposition testimony. This was seen as tampering with evidence and didn't look good. It showed him as a manipulator and liar.

An associate of Forsythe testified that Forsythe had been a courier for Hughes. He testified in part that Forsythe had told him in 1976, "Yes, and from what he said from time to time, I knew that this had been going on for years… It was very strange. He said he had to be on call within reach of a telephone at all times. He always had to leave a number where he could be available, and sometimes long periods of time would go by without a call coming from Mr. Hughes. But when a call came, he had to be available to carry out these errands. He was sort of a private messenger for Mr. Hughes…"

Two witnesses who saw him on April 27, 1976, in Willard, including the big rancher at the gas station, corroborated his testimony.

There was also corroboration through a deposit slip showing a deposit of two thousand eight hundred dollars in one hundred dollar bills into Forsythe's bank account on the day Hughes died. This was the money he said he received in one of the envelopes given to him by Hughes.

The bank teller who waited on him testified that the bills deposited by Forsythe had red seals, which indicated that the money was old. These were brand new bills and had not been used, indicating they originated during the pertinent time period when the will was signed in 1968. A representative of the U.S. Mint testified that $100 bills with red seals were last issued in January 1971.

The physical evidence consisted of the large brown envelope, the will envelope, the visitor's center envelope, a short note, the three-page will, and volumes of Hughes's handwritten memos. The will envelope had a red imprint on the back, over the seal of the envelope. It was imprinted with "LAS VEGAS, NEV, MAR." The day and year were illegible as was the printer number. The actual postage stamped by the postage printer on the envelope was for six cents, the cost of a first-class stamp from January of 1968 through May of 1971. The will was dated March 19, 1968. At the time of the trial in 1977, postage was thirteen cents. The stamp could not have been made after May of 1971.

A Pitney Bowes representative testified that the Desert Inn Hotel had a Pitney Bowes postage printer installed on June 1, 1967. He couldn't say where the printer was actually located in the building.

An FBI document expert testified that the postage meter mark was consistent with a Pitney Bowes postage printer. He testified that the "MAR" designated the month of March, and the "LAS VEGAS, NV" designated the place where it was stamped.

An FBI fingerprint expert testified that the left thumbprint of Melvin Dummar was found on the lower left corner of page

six of the index page in the book *Hoax* (this was a book exposing a phony Hughes biography) obtained from the Weber
State College library. The book included an insert of a Hughes
handwritten memo. Melvin was accused of using the memo
to copy Hughes's handwriting. He testified that he had looked
at the book shortly after receiving the will in 1976 to see if
Hughes's handwriting matched that of the will. It would be
logical for a person to do some research to see if a document's
writing matched that of Howard Hughes. The stakes were certainly high enough for this type of research. On the other
hand, maybe Melvin wanted to duplicate the handwriting if
he forged the will. No fingerprints of Melvin or Bonnie
Dummar or of Howard Hughes were found on the will or the
original envelope containing the will.

My training has taught me that not everyone who touch-
es a document will leave a fingerprint. Fingerprints are
essentially residue of skin oils, dirt, sweat, or other materi-
als picked up on the skin. Since Hughes washed his hands
with alcohol regularly, the skin on his hands would be dry
and relatively free from oils or dirt. Fingerprint identification is an exact science. Each individual has a unique set of
ridges on many surface areas of the skin that can be compared with unknown latent prints and identified as identical
or not identical. No conclusion could be made on the age of
the paper the will was written on.

An Alcohol, Tobacco, and Firearm (ATF) chemist testified that after conducting a thin layer chromatography test,
a test that isolates unique chemical fingerprints for ink, "The
ink on the will came from a ballpoint pen. The ink was manufactured by Paper Mate." He explained there were three
thousand formulas of ink on the market at the time. He continued, "The ink formula was identified as formula number

307. Paper Mate first put this formula on the market in 1963. Formula 307 was discontinued by Paper Mate and was no longer used in its ballpoints after February 1974."

A Hughes aide testified that during the time Hughes lived in the Desert Inn, "I remember, he wrote with a ballpoint pen. And it was a Paper Mate."

"Are you sure?"

"At that period he was using only Paper Mates. We would give 'em to him when he needed them. I bought them by the dozen."

I am by no means an expert on handwriting, but I'm aware that handwriting analysis is not an exact science. The expert, depending on training and experience, uses all of his skill to determine if a certain person has made the unknown handwriting. There are many influencing factors in the analysis: Is there sufficient known handwriting to make a comparison? Are there sufficient identifiable characteristics in the handwriting? Has the person's handwriting changed over time? Is the unknown handwriting disguised? Was the handwriting done under the influence of duress, drugs, or a physical or mental disorder? How much additional evidence is there that the suspected writer is the right person? The expert may be willing to stretch his opinion if he's sure it's the right person. Is the client willing to pay for the opinion? Unfortunately, money is a great motivator to expert witnesses. In the end, the expert's finding is based on his opinion. That's why there are experts who have different opinions regarding the same handwriting. Handwriting identification is best applied as corroborative evidence, and should never be accepted on its own.

Noah Dietrich, the named executor of the will, had been intimately involved with Hughes for years. He was the man who had run Hughes's businesses until 1957. He had been a thirty-six-year-old, hired by a nineteen-year-old, when he first came on with Hughes. At the time of the trial, Dietrich had white hair, was in his late sixties, and in failing health. He used a cane on his walk to the stand. After slowly seating himself, he testified when asked about the handwriting, "All I know is Howard Hughes wrote the will."

The lawyer asked a follow-up question. "What about the handwriting experts who say it's a fake?"

He answered, "What about those who say it isn't?"

"Would you care to comment on the experts who are going to testify that it's a forgery?"

"Only that they might do well to consider another line of work."

There were chuckles from the packed courtroom.

A female handwriting expert who worked on over five hundred cases a year for various law enforcement agencies, and who was the only American testifying for the proponents, testified, "It is my opinion that the writer of the exemplars which were presented to me is the same individual who wrote the questioned will."

The cross-examination took five days and included the following by Freeze: "Isn't it true that you looked at the questioned will, picked out a feature, and then began searching through hundreds of exemplars until you found a similar feature?"

"No, that is not true. I examined the exemplars first."

In his arrogance, Freeze broke one of the principle rules for cross-examination. He asked a question he didn't already know the answer to. "Was there a time, after your examination of the original will, when you considered not testifying for the proponents?"

"Yes."

"Wasn't that because you had reason to believe it was a forgery and you didn't want to be discredited?"

"That was not the reason I hesitated. I hesitated because somebody was trying to intimidate me. I was asked not to testify."

"By whom?"

"By someone in a high official position in my profession."

"You mean to tell us that you were threatened?"

"Not with physical harm, no. But it was an intimidation nevertheless. I was told that if I testified in the Howard Hughes trial—and these were the words used—against one of our own,' that I would never be accepted by my colleagues in this country. And that it would be very difficult for me to continue in this profession. But I felt that I had to do what was right, and I am here."

I don't blame the contestants for fighting against the will. Melvin's allegations were too remarkable to believe. It's doubtful the contestants had anything to do with the blacklisting threats. It appears it was strictly done to protect the ego and reputation of the president of the U.S. Handwriting Association.

The proponents weren't able to convince any other American handwriting experts to look at the will. Apparently the threat of blacklisting was well known in the U.S. handwriting community.

A Dutch handwriting expert testified for seven days regarding similarities in the known handwriting of Hughes and the handwriting of the will. He was asked, "Back to the will. Was it written with good control?"

The man paused thoughtfully. "In various places in the questioned will, it appears as though the hand of the writer went out of control. This indicates some disturbance of motor coordination."

Rhoden asked, "From your examination of the questioned will and these hundreds of exemplars of writing of Howard Hughes, do you have an opinion as to who wrote the questioned will?"

The witness smiled. "I have. I am convinced that the man who wrote the exemplars, whom I am told was Howard Hughes, is the man who wrote the questioned will."

"Do you have any doubt about that?"

"I'm certain of that beyond any reasonable doubt."

"Is it possible for it to have been a forgery?"

"No, of course not."

The expert was cross-examined for two days regarding inconsistencies in Hughes's handwriting, and example after example was put forward attempting to refute his testimony.

A French expert, who required a translator, testified for a day and concluded that, "The questioned document was written by Howard Hughes."

Rhoden questioned, "How sure are you?"

"I know in my soul and conscience that this is so."

The cross-examination covered inconsistencies in Hughes's writing of various letters.

Another French expert also testified. After being asked if it was difficult to come to a conclusion, he responded, "It was easy for me."

"What made it easy?"

"Because there is an abundance of similarities for comparison in the exemplars of writing of Mr. Hughes."

"Even though you say you are one hundred percent certain that Howard Hughes wrote the questioned will, would you leave room for some small doubt?"

"There is no room, my good sir, for any doubt, even the smallest. I am certain, and on this certainty, I would stake my life."

There was no cross-examination.

An FBI expert testified that he found the will to be a forgery. Under cross-examination he was asked, "Can handwriting experts form opposite opinions concerning the genuineness of a document and both be honest?"

"Yes, experts many times disagree on a particular document, and they can do so honestly."

A deposition was read into the record stating that another expert found the will to be "... a very poorly concocted, simulated forgery."

In cross-examination during the deposition, this witness stated that he was already aware of the opinion of the president of a prestigious American handwriting association prior to his one-hour examination of the will.

Another deposition of a female expert was read into the record. She determined that the will was a forgery based on conversations with the same president. She stated that she had come to her conclusion "... primarily by examining the original will alone..." She testified that she found indicators of forgery in "... unusual places where the pen is lifted, and retracing. Whenever these appear, sir, the work is a forgery."

The president of the handwriting organization, who had testified in hundreds of cases, worked in a crime lab for a large sheriff's department, and later, worked for private attorneys and insurance companies, testified that the will was a "... rank forgery. Rank!"

"Are you able to tell us, after examining Dummar's handwriting, if it was written by Melvin Dummar?"

"I cannot tell you that the forger was Dummar. But I can tell you that this forgery is a slavish copy. The line quality is slow. There is patching, unnatural pen lifts. There isn't the natural variation in letters, which everyone has in his handwriting, and that's a dead giveaway. This is a rank forgery."

This expert also testified that the Pitney Bowes imprint on the back of the envelope was a forgery. Under cross-examination, numerous points were brought up to impeach his testimony on this point, but he held fast to his opinion.

A retired FBI handwriting expert, who admitted being friends with the previous expert, testified that the will was a forgery. He disagreed with the opinion that the Pitney Bowes stamp was a forgery.

An expert from Chicago testified, "... I found that in the name Howard R. Hughes, the first name and the middle initial are traced. They were traced from a signature on page one of the answers to interrogatories published in the book *Hoax*."

He was asked, "First, how can this tracing be accomplished?"

"The forger places the model over a glass table with light coming from underneath, tracing the signature by placing the paper on which the writing is traced over the copy."

"Was the last name also traced?"

"No, it was a freehand attempt imitation."

During cross-examination, he admitted that the will itself did not appear to be traced, but he was adamant about the signature of Hughes being a tracing.

I thought it was strange that only the first and middle name would be traced, but the last name as well as the body of the will would be forged freehand.

Hughes's personal aides were designated hostile witnesses by the proponents because of their uncooperative behavior. All of them testified that Hughes never left the Desert Inn Hotel during the time he resided in Las Vegas.

Robert Maheu (chief of Las Vegas operations) testified that he had daily telephone contact with Hughes. He stated that he "... could not say categorically that Hughes had not slipped out of the Desert Inn" during the period of time that Melvin reportedly picked up Hughes, but he was convinced that he hadn't left his room. Maheu also testified that Hughes, on occasion, made many of the same misspellings as were found in the will.

A tax attorney testified that he had conversed with various Hughes aides over the telephone during the pertinent time period in 1967. He was asked, "How did you communicate with Mr. Hughes about this matter?"

The attorney responded, "One of his aides on duty would phone me and read to me, word for word, a memo Mr. Hughes had written. Then the aide would take down, word for word, my answer."

"At any time in the month of December 1967, did you speak to Howard Hughes himself on the telephone?"

"No."

"On the twenty-ninth of December, after seven o'clock Houston time—five o'clock Las Vegas time—did you have any further contact with anyone on the ninth floor of the Desert Inn?"

"No."

During the probate trial, various aides testified about Hughes. They provided an interesting insight into the man. John Holmes (now deceased), one of the aides, when asked where Hughes spent his time at the Desert Inn, responded, "In his bedroom, in bed, or in the bathroom." When asked if Hughes could have left the ninth floor through the fire escape, he said no, because "... if Mr. Hughes had left by the fire-escape door, any aide on duty would have heard him because the back door had a noisy bolt. We tested the door to see how it worked, and it made quite a racket."

Roy Crawford (now deceased), another aide, was asked, "Could anyone on the ninth floor have used the back door to leave without the guard stationed at the elevator seeing him?"

"Yes."

"Was there a bolt on the back door?"

"Yes."

"Did you ever work the bolt?"

"Yes."

"Was it noisy or quiet?"

"There wasn't anything noisy about it. I tried it myself."

Holmes committed perjury regarding the lock noise. Crawford and others testified the lock was silent. This was a material fact in the trial because it was evidence that Hughes could have slipped out unnoticed by the guards.

Crawford was kept on at Hughes Tool Company after Hughes's death, with an increase in salary, and was guaranteed a lifetime consulting job. He was banished from the inner circle because he had broken the code of silence by cooperating with Maheu. He was kept on the payroll in order to secure his loyalty.

Howard Eckersley (now deceased) testified that he earned seventy-five thousand dollars to ninety-five thousand dollars a year plus ten thousand dollars to twenty thousand dollars as an "executive staff assistant." This was a substantial income at the time. Eckersley's duties were "... to see to the needs of Mr. Hughes." It was learned that these needs included storing his urine in bottles, and other utterly mundane duties, as well as looking after the personal needs of their sovereign. He also testified that he had been on duty on December twenty-sixth, twenty-seventh, twenty-eighth, twenty-ninth, and thirtieth, 1967. He testified that Hughes never left the Desert Inn during that time.

A memo was read to Eckersley when he was on the witness stand. The attorney stated, "Here's a memo written by Hughes during the Desert Inn period." Rhoden read part of the document. "'I feel better doing something highly secret like this when Howard was on and it is at night.' What was the highly secret thing that Mr. Hughes did while at the Desert Inn?"

Eckersley squirmed as he answered, "I don't remember."

Hughes executive assistants, more accurately described as personal body aides, all testified in the trial. These men were on duty with Hughes twenty-four hours a day. In fact they were the only people who saw him face-to-face with very few exceptions. The aides swore under oath to testify truthfully. Nevertheless, they gave totally contradictory testimony on such a simple fact as whether or not Hughes had long hair while residing in Las Vegas. This would seem to be a trivial matter at first glance, but it goes to the heart of Melvin's testimony about the description of the old man he rescued in the desert.

One of the aides, Roy Crawford, testified that Hughes had a beard and hair well below his shoulders, with long fingernails and toenails during the time he resided at the Desert Inn Hotel in Las Vegas.

Another member of the personal guards, John Holmes, also testified that he had begun working for Hughes in 1949 as a driver. He was made a personal assistant in 1957. Holmes was asked if Hughes had long hair while living at the Desert Inn. He responded, "Certainly not."

He was asked, "Did his hair reach his shoulders?"

His response was, "That's ridiculous! Never!"

Gordon Margulis, a cocky Englishman, testified that he had come to Las Vegas in 1967 and had applied for a busboy job. He had assumed that busboy meant driving a bus. He added some comic relief to the trial, but at the same time showed how things worked inside Hughes's inner sanctum. His duties as a busboy included delivering food to the no-man's land of the ninth floor penthouse. For some reason someone liked the way he delivered food, and he was hired as a cook, even though he had never cooked anything in his life. Margulis was asked, "Then how were you able to cook?"

He responded with a smile, "It was easy. The cook didn't cook. All I had to do was warm up Mr. Hughes's food. He'd eat some canned soup, and when he'd stop for a while, it'd get cold, and he'd want it warmed up, so I'd warm it up. He'd want the same soup warmed up again, so I'd warm it up again. This'd go on for hours with the same soup. My title was cook, but I was really a warmer."

Margulis identified Hughes's personal aides as John Holmes, Roy Crawford, Chuck Waldron, Levar Myler, George Francom, and Howard Eckersley. He was also asked if Hughes could have left the Desert Inn without the guards knowing about it. He responded, "Oh sure. Why not? It was possible for anyone to've gotten out without bein' noticed. All he had to do was go to the back door an' open it an' go down the stairs."

Gordon Margulis also testified after being asked by Freeze, "After this will showed up, did you tell anyone that in your opinion it was a forgery?"

"Sure."

"Isn't that because you know that Mr. Hughes never left the Desert Inn to have been picked up by Melvin Dummar?"

"How do I know if he left the Desert Inn? I wasn't up there every night. How do I know what he did or didn't do when I wasn't there?"

"On what did you base your opinion that the will was a forgery."

"Oh, the fact that the name Spruce Goose was in it. I always had the impression that Mr. Hughes didn't like that name. An' I read in the newspapers that everyone said it was a forgery."

"Your opinion has changed, has it?"

"Well, I'm not so sure anymore."

"What has made you not so sure anymore?"

"What I keep readin' in the newspapers. All of a sudden we have one guy sayin' he never kept a log in the Desert Inn, an' I know they kept logs there. An' one guy says Mr. Hughes had short hair, an' another guy says it was long. One guy says his toenails were too long for him to wear shoes, an' another guy says he wore shoes all the time walkin' to the bathroom... All I know is there is a lot of lyin' goin' on here... I know that John Holmes used to tell me that the boss had a handwritten will an' that he gave it to somebody to hold for 'I'm in secret, an' that the aides didn't know who had it, an' that they wanted to know. Then up pops this handwritten will, an' some guy says that Hughes gave it to him to hold in secret, an' now everybody's trying to say that this isn't the will. Well, I ain't so sure it ain't his will."

I was able to speak with Margulis. He's still a feisty Englishman. He said that he hasn't had contact with any of the Hughes aides for many years, but he doubted that they would be of much help, if they were still alive. He explained that their lifetime consulting contracts continued in force even after William Lummis took over Summa Corporation. They would have no incentive to cooperate as they would forfeit their substantial retirement contracts.

• • •

Harold Rhoden stood before the witness. He was becoming exasperated. It had been a long day, and the witness wasn't cooperating. He stood, stoop shouldered and wearied; his rumpled blue suit speaking volumes about his state of mind. Finally, after taking a deep breath, he asked his next question. "The next morning, at the Mizpah Hotel, did you notice something unusual in the lobby?"

"Well, there was a certain amount of excitement there in the lobby, and four or five gentlemen told me. They were going crazy. There was a lot of commotion. Everybody was running around sort of confused and upset."

"What did they say to you?"

"Well, I—they told me they were trying to locate Mr. Hughes. That's all they told me. And I remember saying, 'Well, when you find him, let me know, and I'll buy him a beer!'"

Edwin Daniel (believed to be deceased), testified reluctantly and had to be pressed relentlessly to cooperate. He testified he had been in Tonopah, Nevada, on a trip when he saw John Meier at the Mizpah Hotel along with some other Hughes employees. He described the employees as mining consultants or engineers, and not personal aides. Daniel, director of engineering for the Frontier Hotel, admitted to being a friend of Kay Glenn, the supervisor of Hughes's personal aides. This was probably one reason why he didn't want to testify. Glenn had testified that Hughes never left the Desert Inn. Daniel testified that the incident at the Mizpah occurred some time in 1967. He couldn't pin down the exact time, other than to say he knew it was after the month of August of that year. Later, he hedged about the year, and said it could have been 1968, 1969, or 1970.

Daniel had met with attorney Rhoden the night before and told his story without any hesitation, but he appeared at trial the next morning with bruises and cuts on his face. Were his injuries a result of a beating to encourage him to amend his story? There were many who didn't want his story to be told in court.

Daniel squirmed on the stand. His altered face was evidence of an incident that had occurred between the time he was interviewed the evening before and the morning of his testimony. He was very hard to pin down in his answers. In his frustration and anger, he glared contemptuously at the lawyer as if he were looking at something he had stepped in. The witness was being crushed between two alternatives. If he testified truthfully, he could get another beating, or maybe worse. He was stuck! He had to take the stand. The only solution for him was to walk a thin line between telling the complete truth and telling a lie. He was forced by circumstance to water down his testimony, so that he would satisfy both the court and his attackers.

Rhoden knew what was happening, but he had to continue his questioning. "At the Mizpah Hotel, when you saw John Meier in the lobby with a group of men, did you say to Meier, referring to one of the group, 'Is that who I think it is?'"

"No, I didn't say nothing like that to him!"

"Last night in your lawyer's office didn't you tell me that is exactly what you asked John Meier, and that he answered, 'Yes, it is?'"

"No, I didn't tell you that!"

"All right, and it was after you were looking at those men that you think you might have made this statement, asked this question, something like, 'Is that who I think it is?'"

"If I recall that exactly, when certain parties or associates of Mr. Meier walked over to the bar in which I was sitting, they made a remark that that was Mr. Hughes. I don't believe I asked the question, but I may have. I don't recall."

"The next morning at the Mizpah Hotel, did you notice something in the lobby?"

"To the best of my recollection, there was a certain amount of excitement there in the lobby of the hotel in which I was having a beer or two, and whoever was in the group, four or five gentlemen in the group told—I asked them what they were excited about, and they told me."

The fact that Daniel was having "a beer or two" in the morning tells us a bit about him.

Rhoden continued his questioning, "Did they say something like this, 'The old man is missing and we can't find him?'"

Daniel's mind was racing. He responded, "I can't remember."

"Did you tell a state investigator, in substance, 'I was at the Mizpah Hotel in Tonopah one morning, the Summa people were around, everyone was going crazy, there was a lot of commotion going on, people were running around very confused and upset, and I said, "What is the problem?" asking Johnny Meier, and Meier said, 'Well, the old man is lost or gone from the Mizpah Hotel?'"

"I don't recall saying that to the gentleman, exactly that."

At this point, a letter from a Nevada Deputy Attorney General was read into the record. The letter, in part, stated,

"... Mr. Daniel stated that John Meier informed him that Howard Hughes was lost in the Tonopah area for two or three days about the time Melvin Dummar claims he picked up Mr. Hughes and drove him back to Las Vegas."

The investigator for the state, who had interviewed Daniel, took the stand next. He was asked to "... tell us the words he (Daniel) used."

"He was at the Mizpah Hotel in Tonopah, Nevada, and the Hughes people were running around, and there seemed to be a lot of confusion, and he asked Johnny Meier, (he referred to him as Johnny Meier), what the problem was, and he said the old man was missing. I believe he used lost."

Daniel testified that he didn't know when these events at the Mizpah Hotel had occurred, but he thought it was some time after August of 1967, because the Frontier Hotel was completed in August of that year, and he was employed at the Frontier as chief engineer. He also said that he had been directed to go to the Mizpah regarding mining claim properties by someone from Hughes Tool Company. He wasn't asked who sent him. Another inexplicable flaw in the questioning was that Daniel was never asked who he meant when he stated, "Is that who I think it is?"

The fact that he hedged on this identification is indicative of his fear of putting Hughes at the Mizpah. From the total content of his testimony, he was obviously referring to Howard Hughes. He also wasn't asked who the "... four or five gentlemen..." with Meier were. If they were mining consultants, they could have been Leonard Traynor, Clarence Hall, Dennis Hill, and Eldon Cleveland (all deceased). These were the men who sold mines to Hughes Tool Company over and over again.

Records show that Hughes bought the Frontier Casino

on December 23, 1967. If Daniel had been told to go to the Mizpah by someone from Hughes Tool Company, then it would have had to be after Hughes acquired the Frontier. He testified that he had been told to go there regarding some mining claims. His travel to Tonopah had to have occurred after the twenty-third, probably after the holidays.

Hughes always used aliases when he was engaged in something he wanted to keep secret. He used an alias when he got married, when he moved into the Desert Inn, and on other occasions. In all likelihood, he and his crew used aliases when staying at the Mizpah.

During the probate trial, Kay Glenn was queried, "Did you ever say anything to Dr. Ford that Hughes would take off into the desert without his aides having knowledge of his whereabouts, and once when Mr. Hughes was out there, something happened and he was picked up and brought back to Las Vegas?"

Glenn responded angrily, "I never said anything like that to Dr. Ford!"

I was able to locate Dr. Jonathon Ford, a retired dentist who is married to a cousin of Kay Glenn. Although he no longer practices, he leases his dental office to another dentist. As I pulled up to the building, Ford was out sweeping the driveway. In spite of his retirement, he keeps active. I introduced myself and explained my purpose. He informed me that after he had testified in the probate trial, he had learned that Glenn had been very upset with him for testifying regarding a conversation he had been part of. He told me that he stood by his sworn deposition he had given in 1977. The deposition was read into the court record during the trial as rebuttal to Glenn's testimony.

Ford swore that he and his father-in-law and their wives

attended a dental convention in Las Vegas in early November of 1970. They had dinner with Glenn at the Desert Inn. During the course of the dinner, either Glenn or his father-in-law, based on what Glenn had told him (he wasn't sure which), stated that, "Hughes would take off in the desert without the aides having knowledge of his whereabouts," and that "Mr. Hughes had gone out in the past to the desert and something happened out there, and he was picked up and brought back to Las Vegas by someone passing in a car."

Ford would have had no reason to concoct this story. He was essentially a disinterested party, and by testifying he provided evidence that went against a relative's story.

John Henderson (now deceased), a weathered horseman who looked like he had ridden out of a western movie, was riding with his wife and son near American Flat, southwest of Virginia City, Nevada in late 1967.

Virginia City is a turn of the century mining town, preserved as a tourist attraction. It's a narrow cleft in a mountainside lined with multi-story frame and brick buildings. The mountains are cinnamon and brown sugar colored. The area south of this region is perfect for horseback riding. American Flat is two hundred and twenty miles north of Tonopah.

The riders had been out for several hours in the northern desert enjoying the scenery. Henderson stated he saw an elderly man walking alone on a dirt road leading to an abandoned mine, miles away from civilization. Henderson didn't see a car or a horse. He thought the man might need help, so he left his wife and son and rode down a hill to the man. When Henderson reached the man, he asked him if he needed help. The man grunted, "No."

The man was carrying a paper sack in one hand and a walking stick in the other. He was walking toward some abandoned mines. He had a mustache and was about six feet tall. Henderson said, "He wore an old felt hat and street shoes—not the kind you wear in the desert. His clothes looked like secondhand clothes. When he looked up at me, I recognized him. It was Howard Hughes."

As Henderson rode off, he noticed a car in the distance. He described it as a late model Chrysler. Henderson's testimony sounds credible. He had no stake in the outcome of the trial, and his description of Hughes fits. His testimony shows that Hughes was out of the Desert Inn and in the area of western Nevada near some mines.

Another piece of the puzzle was put together at the trial when, during his testimony, Kay Glenn was asked, "During the Desert Inn period, did Mr. Hughes own a Chrysler?"

He answered, "Yes."

What would a man walking in the desert be doing with a paper bag? Was it his lunch? Was he picking up trash? Or could the answer be that Hughes was seldom without a paper bag, as he often discarded his used Kleenex tissues in it. Henderson wouldn't have known about this fact, as only the aides were aware of it. Also, how would Henderson know that Hughes had a Chrysler? If the man was Hughes, the chance meeting with Henderson would, in all likelihood, have occurred before or after December 29, 1967 because Melvin picked up the old man on the twenty-ninth. It's also possible that Hughes may have visited the mining areas more than once. The overriding question is, If the man was Hughes, why was Hughes out in the middle of nowhere walking toward abandoned mines?

I specifically asked Mell Stewart (Hughes's barber) what

kind of cars were available for the use of the aides. He explained, "The aides had access to the seven to twelve cars as needed. They were Mercedes, Buicks, and Chryslers. He liked Chryslers."

William Gay, Chester Davis (corporate attorney), and Nadine Henley (Hughes's former secretary) ran Hughes's empire when he died. In December of 1972, Hughes Tool Company went public and began doing business as Summa Corporation. Control of Summa essentially went to Gay.

Frank William Gay, the power behind the Hughes throne, testified that he had started working for Hughes in 1947 as a part-time errand boy. He rose in the ranks and eventually ended up running the Hughes operations. When asked by Freeze during the trial if there was a chance that Hughes had left the Desert Inn and gone out in the desert without any of the aides telling him, he responded, "Oh, there is a possibility they would not have told me, yes. It depends upon who was with him."

Freeze stumbled again by asking the question one more time. "Mr. Gay, listen carefully to my question. If Mr. Hughes had been wandering around in the desert and had been injured, don't you think it would have been known by the officers of the company?"

Gay didn't hesitate. He responded, "I think it is quite possible he could have left his room at the Desert Inn, and they're not telling me."

The contestants' evidence included handwriting experts, attacks on Dummar and Forsythe, and the testimony of aides who said emphatically that Hughes never left the Desert Inn.

In his opening statement, Freeze promised to prove that Bonnie Dummar forged the Mormon Will. He also promised to prove that Melvin was in a conspiracy with her and LeVane Forsythe. In the end, he did no such thing. The assurances were nothing more than a scrap yard of promises. He used smoke and mirrors in an attempt to smother the jury with unfulfilled promises. These statements stuck in the jurors' minds, but by the end of the eight-month trial, the promises were long un-kept.

The proponents had spent one-quarter of a million dollars on the trial. They should have used more of it for additional investigators. The contestants spent three million. There were approximately one hundred witnesses called to testify. Closing arguments ended on June 5, 1978 at 4:30 P.M. The jury's verdict was returned on June 8, 1978 at 7:30 P.M.

After eight months of trial testimony and literally pounds of document evidence, the jury deliberated for only eleven hours. The proponent team was absolutely sure they had won. Judge Hayes asked, "Members of the jury, have you reached a verdict?"

Juror number five, the foreman, responded, "We have."

The clerk of the court read the verdict. "We, the jury, find that the purported three-page will dated March 19, 1968 was not written by Howard R. Hughes."

There was a gasp from many of the spectators, and the assembled reporters broke for the pay phones and cameras. In spite of the verdict, there was no evidence presented as to who forged the will. Melvin and his wife were never charged with any crime or even accused of forging the will.

Judge Hayes, before passing away from cancer approximately a year and a half after the trial ended, told a friend he was most looking forward to reuniting with his mother, and then he wanted to meet Howard Hughes. He said he had a question he wanted to ask him.

It's interesting that William Lummis was in a win-win situation with regard to the will, as he was a named inheritor and would have received one-sixteenth of Hughes's estate if the will were found to be legitimate. Lummis went for all the marbles when he, through his mother, contested the will and hit the jackpot.

After huge income taxes, estate taxes, and penalties were paid, Lummis and the other relatives ended up inheriting the Hughes estate. Lummis took over Summa Corporation and moved his family to Las Vegas. He learned that Summa had been mishandled and that the Hughes casinos were losing money. After an extended court battle with Bill Gay and his cohorts, Lummis won control. He was named administrator of the estate and assumed management. He sold the casinos and other Las Vegas holdings, and Summa Corporation went into the real estate development business. Lummis retired in 1990.

On June 12, 1996, Summa Corporation, which consisted of Howard Hughes Corporation, Howard Hughes Properties LP/Inc., and Summerlin Corporation, merged into the F.S. Rouse Company. Virtually all of Hughes's assets are located in Las Vegas. F.S. Rouse Company's taxable assets in 2004 were $938,456,506. The company was merged into General Growth Properties on November 12, 2004. General Growth Properties is the second largest U.S. publicly traded real estate investment trust and operates in forty-four states.

6

The Old Man

T here are two questions at the heart of this mystery. The one considered in the trial looked primarily at the authenticity of the will. The second question is: Did Melvin Dummar pick up Howard Hughes in the desert of Nevada on that cold, dark December night? That question was addressed at the trial, but inconsistently and ineffectively.

Melvin is the key to this riddle. His story was the spark that ignited this fire. I needed to hear the story from his lips. I had to assess him and attempt to punch holes in his remarkable tale. After a good deal of research, my investigation began with him.

Melvin lives near Promontory Summit on the north end of the Great Salt Lake in Utah. The Great Salt Lake is the largest inland lake outside of the Great Lakes. Because of the extended drought in the West, the lake has dropped to its lowest level since 1967, the same year Melvin said he picked up Howard Hughes.

Over one hundred years ago, a golden spike was driven into the tracks completing the nation's first transcontinental railroad line at Promontory Summit. By the end of 1869, Promontory was full of gamblers, outlaws, and con men. Passengers traveling west on the Central Railroad had to disembark and wait for the arrival of the Union Pacific train to continue their travel to California. Canvas and rough-hewn lumber shacks accommodated the travelers while they waited. They drank, gambled, and wasted away their time like prisoners waiting for a commutation of sentence.

This area is also the home of the Bear River Marsh, a huge expanse of seventy-four thousand acres of wetlands and mud flats, and home to hundreds of thousands of waterfowl. Melvin has finally left the confines of the Nevada desert and has moved to a lush, abundant place.

He resides in a manufactured home set on a slight hillside. Large trees surround the house that fronts on a sheer mountain. The rear of the home overlooks pastures and marshland. As I looked out of his large picture window to the west I could see horses grazing in the distance and ducks trading back and forth on the horizon. When I was there, the mountains were covered by early June grass.

Melvin invited me in to the well-kept and comfortable home, and we seated ourselves on sofas in the living room. He seemed relaxed and was very pleasant. The first thing I noticed about him was his bald head. He explained that he was undergoing chemotherapy treatments at the University of Utah Cancer Center in preparation for a bone marrow transplant. He said he had stomach tumors and the cancer had invaded his lymphatic system. The therapy had weakened him and caused his hair to fall out. He was sublimely optimistic and didn't dwell on his health problems. He discussed his physical condition as though he were talking about going to the dentist for a teeth cleaning. Melvin reached up with his right hand and rubbed his head as he talked. He reiterated, "I just want the truth to come out."

During the interview he laughed frequently. On one occasion, he became emotional and broke down sobbing when he recounted how Judge Hayes had threatened him with jail if he lied during his deposition. I found his memory to be good, and his story was consistent throughout. Melvin looked surprisingly healthy. He wasn't gaunt or thin as you would expect for someone undergoing cancer treatment. He dressed in cowboy style clothes, and some have described him as a Glenn Campbell look-alike.

I told Melvin, "It's very important to tell me the complete truth about the events of December 29, 1967. I know it was a long time ago and memories fade and our minds sometimes play tricks on us by remembering things that didn't really occur as we recall them. If you can't remember, just say you can't remember. Above all, don't make up facts."

He responded immediately, "I didn't ask you here so I could make up stuff."

His hand went to his head again. This time he rubbed more vigorously. He noticed my questioning gaze and quickly explained.

"The chemo makes my head itch; it drives me crazy."

I wanted the whole story told from his mouth. I wanted to analyze each detail and hopefully elicit a few new facts. He had told the story many times before, but never to an investigator. He said the tale began when he lived in Gabbs, Nevada in 1967. He was twenty-three years of age at the time.

The thought struck me. Twenty-three is young for an

unsophisticated country boy to have enough foresight to plant a seed about picking up Hughes. Then, he would have to be ever so patient by letting the seed lay dormant for years until Hughes died so he could come forward with the will. This seemed to be quite a stretch, especially since Melvin is impetuous by nature.

Melvin worked like a dog at a mine filling bags with magnesium. His wife, Linda, had left him for another man, and then when things didn't work out, she had gone to live with her mother in California. Linda had a history of running off with other men. She had been a stripper and had no resistance to a friendly smile and sweet talk. During her marriage to Melvin, she often received mail from other men and sometimes corresponded with her new lovers.

Melvin was young and immature and was willing to look the other way to a point, but when the love letters started it became too much. He was driven mad by her actions and developed a system of opening her mail without her knowledge. He would read the mail and then reseal the envelope without her finding out. He learned that this made him even crazier, and he confronted her with the facts. This caused huge eruptions of anger on both sides.

He had spent Christmas of 1967 with his family in Gabbs, Nevada. Gabbs is a tiny lifeboat in a sea of pale green sage. It sits on a hillside overlooking a vast, flat valley. From its vantage point, distance is irrelevant, nothing but an inconvenience. There is a grocery store, a restaurant, a bar, and a gas station, all huddled together as if seeking solace. The name "Dummars" is faded and barely visible on the front stucco wall of the service station. The hamlet is a company town. An open pit magnesium mine, located higher on the hillside, dominates the economy. Every resident is somehow connected to the mine. It's understandable how a strain of cabin fever could crush the souls of some of the inhabitants.

Melvin felt uneasy and stifled. He didn't care for sitting around much, so two days after Christmas he took his off-road motorcycle out to the desert for a ride. Sometimes destiny turns on small hinges because, unknown to him at the time, this simple action was about to unalterably change his life forever. He rode hard across the surface of the desert, speeding past sagebrush and scrub. He loved to ride alone and free. He rode along his favorite dirt road and sped as if he were the wind. As he came over a slight hill, he lost control of the bike. He was separated from the machine and found himself diving toward the ground. He hit and skidded along the rough road on his face. The road rash was severe, and fearing broken bones, he went to the hospital where he stayed overnight for observation.

After being released the next day, Melvin walked into his supervisor's office unannounced. When the man saw Melvin he exclaimed, "What happened to you? It looks like somebody took sandpaper to your face." His supervisor was afraid he would develop an infection working at the mine, so he told Melvin to take a couple of weeks off to allow his face to heal.

Melvin was anxious to patch up his marriage with Linda, so he decided to use his sick time to travel to California. I informed him that I had determined that the twenty-ninth of December 1967, was a Friday. He said that would tie down the date he left because he recalled that he departed Gabbs on a Friday. He explained that he left at about 5:00 P.M. and started south. The sun was just setting as he got underway.

The Nevada desert is a lonely place, and the distance passes slowly as there are no landmarks in the blackness. There are no streetlights and few towns. The only focal point is the car headlights penetrating the night. The road is mesmerizing, and it's very easy to fall asleep at the wheel. This stretch of road has claimed many lives over the years.

He pulled into Tonopah, Nevada, about one hundred miles south of Gabbs. He needed to stretch and take a break from driving. He stopped at the largest building in town, the Mizpah Hotel and Casino. He needed to use the rest room, so after relieving himself, the draw of the blackjack tables was too much for him to resist. He played "twenty-one" for a while, winning some, but mostly losing. He told me that he couldn't know how long he spent in the casino because, "It's hard to tell as time disappears when you're gambling. Besides there aren't any clocks in casinos."

A tantalizing probability is that on the night that Melvin stopped at the Mizpah Casino to play blackjack, Hughes had left the same hotel before Melvin arrived. The next morning Hughes was discovered to have wandered off, and his associates were going nuts trying to find him.

It was getting late. Melvin estimated it was between nine and eleven, but there was no way to be sure of the time. He continued driving south on Highway 95 in his blue 1966 Chevrolet Caprice. He plunged into the darkness, barely noticing as he passed through Goldfield, a once prosperous mining town that had fallen on hard times. The few lights from some gas stations and houses flickered by as he was swallowed up by the darkness. He continued south past the Cottontail Ranch, a legal brothel located at Lida Junction. Holding to Old West tradition, bordellos are legal in most of Nevada, except in the greater Las Vegas area.

I asked him if he had stopped at the Cottontail bar. I was aware that during that period, Melvin often stopped at small honky-tonks and saloons and charmed the patrons with his singing. He gave a faint smile and chuckled, "No." I had an uneasy feeling about his answer. Was he holding something back? I wasn't sure.

He told me he slowed his car slightly, looking for a place to pull off the highway. Traffic was light, but he wanted a place where he could relieve himself without being seen by passing traffic. Eventually, several miles south, he pulled off on a dirt road. He drove slowly for about one hundred yards, being careful not to high center on the rough terrain.

I have subsequently learned that there was no moon on that night, so the desert was deadly black. Melvin was surrounded by total darkness except for the area illuminated by his headlights. He was about to stop when he noticed something lying in the road ahead. When he drove closer he could see it was a man. The man was lying face down in the right rut of the road. I asked, "Where was his head? Was it toward the highway or away from it?"

Melvin had never been asked this question before. He said, "His head was away from the highway."

Melvin thought he was dead and sat momentarily staring at the body. His mind was racing. What should he do? I asked, "Was his head resting on his outstretched arm or was his face in the dirt?"

He paused momentarily. "I can't remember."

I followed up, "Was there dirt on his face?"

He thought for a moment. "No, I don't remember dirt on his face."

He figured the body was probably that of a bum or a

prospector, drunk and passed out, or he had been beaten up and left to die. Melvin could see the lights of the Cottontail Ranch glowing like a beacon, and he thought that maybe he should drive to it and report the incident. Suddenly there was some movement by the man. It was as if the bright headlights had awakened him. He stirred slightly and tried to push himself up, but his arm strength was insufficient and he continued to lie there, helpless. Melvin rushed from his car and went over to him. He lifted the groggy man and got him to his feet. I asked, "How tall was he?"

Melvin looked at me thoughtfully, "About as tall as me."

I asked, "When you stood him up, how tall was he?"

Melvin is five foot ten, but he said the man was several inches taller. The man was weak and trembling. The desert was cold, and Melvin was sure he would have died there alone from exposure as the temperature continued to drop. "About how much did the guy weigh?" I asked.

He answered that the man was thin and gaunt and weighed less than one hundred and fifty pounds. Melvin added that he was used to lifting one hundred-pound bags of magnesium and "the old guy didn't weigh much more than a bag."

I instructed Melvin, "I know you've told this story a million times, but see if you can picture in your mind what he wore."

"It's so long ago," he said. After some thought, he proceeded. He said the stranger wore a long sleeved light brown or beige cotton shirt. His trousers were dress slacks and looked to be too large for him. The desert bum didn't have a coat or jacket in the frigid temperature, and Melvin wondered if he had a car somewhere close by, or if someone had just dumped him there on the road. It was conceivable that a car was there, hidden in the blackness out of headlight range. The man had a five or six-day growth of beard and his gray-brown hair was shaggy and fell just above his shoulders. He looked to be between sixty-five and seventy years of age.

"His pants looked like he had pulled them out of some trash bin," explained Melvin.

This didn't make sense to me. Why would the man be jacketless on a cold winter night so far from civilization? Melvin said the bum wore tennis shoes, but Melvin didn't notice a ring or watch or other jewelry. They made their way slowly to the car, Melvin supporting him for the thirty-foot walk. In the light of the Caprice, Melvin noticed dried blood caked on the man's left ear. There was blood soaked into the stranger's shirt collar, on his left shoulder, and down the arm slightly. There were no other signs of external trauma, but it appeared that the blood had come from inside the man's ear. Melvin thought the old-timer "had been smacked in the head with something." This reinforced Melvin's theory that he had been assaulted.

I questioned, "Was the blood wet and shiny, or was it dry?"

He answered, "It was completely dry."

A question struck me. If Melvin was fabricating the story about picking up Hughes, how would he have known what Howard Hughes actually looked like in 1967, when no one outside Hughes's immediate circle knew this information? Hughes hadn't been seen in public for many years, and no photos had been taken of him since 1952. Evidence developed years later showed Melvin's description to be accurate. Did he have inside information? Was it pure luck, a coincidence, or was the man actually Hughes?

Melvin looked over at his passenger, and spoke to the man for the first time. "We need to get you to a hospital."

The man looked straight ahead as if in a trance. He responded immediately. "No, I'm all right. No doctors."

Thinking the derelict had been assaulted, Melvin continued, "We need to tell the police about this."

Another immediate response, "No police."

Melvin realized that although the old guy was trembling, he seemed alert and in control of his mind. He started the Chevrolet and turned up the heat in the car. "You really should see a doctor for that bleeding. You've lost a lot of blood. I can't leave you here."

The man continued staring straight ahead as if avoiding eye contact, but he responded immediately. "No doctors. Just take me to Las Vegas," he said authoritatively.

As they headed for Las Vegas, the stranger kept his gaze on the road ahead. He leaned against the passenger side door, slumped like an exhausted wreck of a man, not responding to the gregarious Dummar's chatter. As the miles passed, Melvin caught the bum staring at him occasionally as if in awe that someone would be doing this for him.

Eventually, the old man's trembling stopped, and he started asking questions about Melvin. Melvin told him that he was on his way to California to see his estranged wife in an effort to patch up their marriage. General conversation continued for a time and Melvin told the man about his job at the Basic Magnesium Mine, and how he had looked for better employment but hadn't had any success. The passenger had no reply. Melvin told the old man that previously, while living in California with his wife, he had applied at several companies including Boeing and Hughes Aircraft.

The man suddenly turned, facing Melvin. It was if he

had been awakened from a trance. "You applied at Hughes?"

Melvin was surprised by the reaction. "Yeah, they said they weren't hiring."

The old man, clearly interested in this line of conversation, responded, "I could get you a job at Hughes."

Melvin almost laughed out loud. He thought to himself, how could this bum get me a job at Hughes Aircraft?

Then the man, as if savoring the moment, dropped a bombshell. With a wry smile he said as a matter of fact, "I could get you a job because I own the company. I'm Howard Hughes."

This was almost more than Melvin could handle. He suppressed a chuckle. He surmised the man must be drunk or had delusions of grandeur. Melvin hadn't smelled any alcohol on his breath, so he concluded the man was a nut. How could Howard Hughes, the wealthiest man in America, look like a vagrant? In Melvin's mind, it wasn't possible. Melvin continued with small talk. He talked about his dream of being a country western singer and his love of writing songs. As he talked, Melvin couldn't help wondering, Who is this guy? The old-timer broke his silence again by asking Melvin his name, and then a short time later he asked it again. He also asked where he was from. Melvin repeated the answers several times. The man was clearly having trouble concentrating. They continued driving south through the endless desert, and as the chatter subsided, it was replaced by country music on the radio.

Melvin and his passenger had driven the one hundred and sixty miles into the black hole of the desert when they saw the bright lights of Las Vegas. The glittering oasis changed the mood immediately. The man now seemed restless. They continued driving south on Highway 95 as it turned into the Las Vegas Strip. The mystery man asked to be dropped off at the Sands Casino, so they drove until they came to the Sands, where Melvin turned left into the parking lot. The passenger said authoritatively, "Take me around back."

Melvin complied and pulled around to the back of the casino. The derelict thanked Melvin for his trouble and got out of the car, then he asked if Melvin had any spare change. Melvin reached in his pocket and pulled out some coins and gave them to him. Melvin assumed that he was like every other bum and would buy a bottle of wine or a cup of coffee with the change. The man thanked him, and then walked away towards the rear of the building. Melvin drove back to the Strip and continued his journey.

Why did the old man ask Melvin for his pocket change when he was dropped off in Las Vegas, and why did he want to be dropped off at the Sands Casino if Hughes lived at the Desert Inn Hotel? The man could have been homeless and lived in Las Vegas, or the answer could be, if it was Howard Hughes, that he realized he was locked out of the Desert Inn penthouse and couldn't get back inside without passing through the casino. The last thing in the world he would have wanted to do was expose himself to someone who might recognize him in his condition. He would have realized that in order to get back to the Desert Inn penthouse he would need help. He needed the change to make a pay phone call to a trusted aide who would pick him up and sneak him up the fire stairwell to return him to the security of his bedroom on the ninth floor. The Sands Hotel and Casino no longer exists. It was razed, and the three thousand-suite mega-resort, The Venetian, has now taken its place.

Melvin was convinced that he had simply helped someone in need and only a small part of him believed the man was actually Howard Hughes. When Melvin arrived in Cyprus, California, near Anaheim, he mentioned the story to his father-in-law, Wayne Sisk (now deceased), and to his wife, Linda. He mentioned it as a point of interest and not as a fact. Sisk, an ex-cab driver, told Melvin, "I was driving my cab in Los Angeles, it was in the forties (1940s), and I picked up Howard Hughes. He wanted to go to some restaurant with some babe." Neither Sisk nor Linda thought the mystery man was actually Hughes. They all laughed about it. It was a ridiculous notion.

Melvin returned to Gabbs with his wife and daughter, but before long, Linda became restless and took off again. This time she went to Hawthorne, Nevada, and then ran off with another man to Las Vegas. She took Melvin's 1966 Caprice with her. Melvin went looking for her in April or May 1968, and located the car parked near the California Club Casino. This was just after the date on the Mormon Will. Melvin found a note on the dashboard addressed to him. It asked, "Did you move to Las Vegas?" It also instructed him to go to a bank and talk to a certain person. Melvin asked Linda about the note. She said it had been in the car for some time, but she had no idea where it came from. Melvin disregarded the message and couldn't remember the name of the bank or the name of the person on the note.

Could it be that Hughes was trying to reach out to Melvin in order to reward him for his good deed? He may have had an underling try to locate Melvin and left instructions for Melvin in his car. We'll never know.

Melvin's marriage to Linda ended, but later he made another impetuous decision by remarrying her. The second marriage was no better than the first, so they finally ended it for good.

I showed two photos of Howard Hughes to Melvin. One was taken of Hughes when he was a pilot and had a mustache. The other was the last known photograph taken of Hughes in 1952. Melvin said both photos resembled the man he picked up, but he was much older and thinner. He also had hair to his shoulders and a somewhat receding hairline. Later, an artist's conception of Hughes was prepared based on Melvin's description.

Hughes's personal barber told me, "While Hughes lived in Las Vegas, he never had his hair cut." The barber spent a good deal of time with Hughes, and he described him as always being naked, with long hair and long fingernails. Hughes often referred to one of his nails as "the screwdriver." The barber was shown an artist's conception of Hughes prepared from a description provided by Melvin. He reported, "Mr. Hughes had longer hair, and he was thinner. The stubble on his face was about right."

George Francom, who had lived with Hughes for years and cared for him during the entire Desert Inn period, was intimately familiar with his boss's appearance. He was shown the artist's conception of Hughes, prepared based on Melvin's description. He stated that it resembled Hughes, but his hair was somewhat shorter, and the beard was a little longer. Investigators know that eyewitnesses often have detail discrepancies when it comes to descriptions. The key point is that the general description given by Melvin fits. This similarity of descriptions is remarkable as Hughes hadn't been seen by anyone but his closest aides while he resided in Las Vegas, and there were no reports of what he looked like until later.

Melvin's story was almost too fantastic to believe, but for some reason it rang true. He didn't seem to be a cunning sort of person or a co-conspirator with dark motives. The stumbling block was the part about the unconscious vagrant identifying himself as Howard Hughes. How was this possible? Was it really Hughes, or was it a derelict pulling Melvin's chain about his identity? In spite of my skepticism, I would try to sort it out.

Melvin was given a polygraph examination before he testified in the trial. The examiner determined that he could not be reliably tested because of his highly emotional nature. The answers to all questions came out as deceptive, even when asked if he lived in Utah (which he did) and if he had a driver's license (which he did). The examiner reported, "Melvin's reaction showed this same crazy deception with the needles going almost off the graph." This certainly isn't a characteristic of a cool, conniving conspirator.

Sometime after the trial, at the urging of a television reporter, Melvin was given another polygraph examination by Dr. Raskin. Raskin found that Melvin was telling the truth and that there was no deception regarding picking up an old man who identified himself as Howard Hughes. He also found that there was no deception when Melvin denied any involvement in writing the will.

One interview of a key witness is seldom sufficient. There is always more to be gleaned, so I met with Melvin again. This time, the rugged Wasatch Mountains, speckled with patches of cedar and aspen trees, were standing like brave soldiers against the winter wind. The grass was brown, and the craggy peaks were snow-covered. The aspens were leafless and naked. They stood in groves like skeletons, as snow began to fall and the temperature dropped like a stone. Melvin looked good. His hair had grown back, and his cancer was in remission. He told me he works when he can, remodeling a house he has purchased. He is easily fatigued. Melvin invited me into his home and handed me a box containing a file about three inches thick. I recognized the pages immediately. They were various FBI reports and memoranda. Melvin had requested his file from the FBI through the Freedom of Information Act. The package had finally arrived.

"Don't waste your time. There's nothing in there of much significance," he remarked dejectedly.

"You're probably right," I responded, "but you never know."

The FBI had located eight hundred and sixty-six pages relating to Melvin. They had sent three hundred and eighty pages and had charged him twenty-eight dollars for copying. The missing pages were said to be investigative documents from other agencies and pages identifying individuals who had provided information. Most pages had the names blacked out.

The report contains pages and pages of laboratory investigative requests submitted by the Nevada Attorney General to the FBI laboratory over a period of time before and during the trial. The Attorney General pursued his hunt for evidence against Melvin. He was convinced that Melvin had committed forgery and fraud. Had he forgotten his agency's interview of Edwin Daniel? The laboratory examinations showed no evidence against Melvin except for the thumbprints they had located on the Mormon Visitor's Center envelope and one page of the *Hoax* book. Melvin admitted to me that he had handled these items. He had a logical explanation for the prints.

Investigators sometimes fall into a trap. This is very easy to do. We can become fixated on a suspect. Experience and training go out the window in a tunnel vision focus. Melvin was seen as a kook. It was assumed he couldn't be telling the truth. Instead of viewing the case with a broad view, the bull's eye was on him. The Attorney General could have benefited from ordering an objective investigation of the entire matter, but that's water under the bridge.

I recall an investigation where I had a photo and descriptive data on a federal fugitive. We went to his mother's home, found him there, and placed him under arrest. The photo matched, as did the scar on his chest. On the way to jail, we received a message over the FBI radio and were told the real fugitive had called and said we had the wrong guy. At first, I thought it was a joke, but then we learned the fugitive had an identical twin who happened to have a scar on his chest also. We went back to the house and picked him up as well. Now we had both twins in handcuffs. After checking their fingerprints we released the first twin. We had picked up the wrong brother even though I was convinced he was our guy. The new facts had changed my whole focus on the case.

I wanted to know why the investigative path regarding Daniel wasn't pursued. The answer to this question could only be obtained by another pilgrimage to western Nevada. On this trip, I drove west on Highway 50. The scenery is more favorable on this drive, but the journey is brutally long. The highway rises and descends as it passes over mountains and valleys. The road is like duct tape stretched tight to the horizon. After several hours, I triumphantly arrived in Eureka, Nevada—"The friendliest town on the loneliest road in America."

I found a little place run by Mennonites. They served home baked bread and made a lovely sandwich. There were five Harley Davidson motorcycles parked outside when I entered. The riders had obviously found the same deli. I continued my sojourn over the next pass when a deafening roar came rushing from the rear. The five Harleys passed on my left; the riders were clothed in black leather with black helmets and visors. They appeared as ferocious beasts of the Apocalypse. They rode in a V formation—four of the riders drafted off the lead rider. They gave me a thumbs-up as they passed.

I was driving in Western Shoshone country. This tribe of Indians roamed this area on their horses long before the ranchers came. They hunted the plentiful game and dominated the region for many years. Much of Highway 50 retraces the route of the Pony Express. These brave riders rode the two thousand miles from St. Joseph, Missouri, to Sacramento, California, beginning in April of 1860. There were thirty Pony Express stations in Nevada.

Before long, I came across a lone bicyclist, his bike burdened with stuffed saddlebags filled with essential gear. He was a solitary pioneer toiling up a seven thousand two hundred-foot peak. I mentally commended him for his bravery. Or was it his insanity?

Suddenly, a coyote appeared about twenty yards off the highway, loping parallel to the road. This is very unusual at midday, but hunger must have driven it to the place to find roadkill. There are many ranchers in this area who would gladly have shot the varmint. Coyotes account for many lamb and calf kills.

As I continued, I noted several white crosses planted as memorials to those who had been sacrificed to the gods of speed. The two-lane highway takes its toll on those who accidentally run off the road in the blackness of the night. Eventually, I saw billboards advertising CPAs and pawnbrokers. This was a sure sign that I had left the wilderness and had entered a more complicated, civilized word. I had arrived in Carson City, the capital of Nevada.

The Attorney General's file on Melvin Dummar is held in the official archives of the state. I reviewed the thick file but was disappointed in what it didn't contain. It consisted of legal filings and other court documents, but there were no letters to the FBI requesting laboratory examinations that I knew existed as a result of my review of an FBI Freedom of Information request. Furthermore, there was no mention of Edwin Daniel's statements to Attorney General personnel. This was irrevocably testified to in the trial. There were no investigative documents. Why wasn't this material in the file, and what else could be missing? I wondered why such an historic file wouldn't be kept intact.

I spoke with the former Chief of the Criminal Division of the Nevada Attorney General's Office who had been assigned to the Hughes probate trial. He said he didn't know what had happened to the missing files. I asked him his opinion of Melvin Dummar. He laughed before responding. "Hughes was a strange guy, but I can't see him willing any money to Dummar. I think Dummar took some facts and put them together to make it look like he would be named in the will. I don't believe Hughes ever left Las Vegas, but he may have. Anything is possible."

The chief investigator for the Attorney General's Office, who has subsequently retired, reminisced about the Hughes case. He informed me he had personally delivered the will and envelopes to FBI agents in Washington D.C. for laboratory examinations. "We had to be very careful with the will. There were a lot of people who wanted to get their hands on it."

He said he had done a great deal of investigation in the Dummar case, and the archives should contain everything he and his team had done. He explained that the Attorney General's Office had "... turned over many times since the trial, and they must have disposed of some of the material for some reason." He continues to hold very strong views about Melvin's complicity in what he referred to as a scam. For example, he had learned during his investigation in Gabbs that Melvin was noted for his ability to cry on cue. He described Melvin as a "... good actor and liar."

There continue to be many intelligent people who believe this. That's exactly why Melvin asked me to conduct this investigation.

I asked about Edwin Daniel at the Mizpah Hotel and why his information was never pursued. He thought for a moment and responded, "I remember something about that, but another investigator interviewed Daniel. I don't know what happened there."

The investigator told me he believes the Pitney Bowes imprint on the will envelope was forged and couldn't be printed by the machine midway down the envelope. If this is true, then it was troubling, and the stamp must be a forgery. I had to resolve this discrepancy, so I reviewed part of the trial testimony.

One of the expert document examiners testified, "First of all, you are not going to be able to put an envelope into a Pitney Bowes machine and get a mark as far down as this one appears on the envelope. The image is about a third of the way down, too far down to have been made by a Pitney Bowes machine."

He continued, "... it isn't a bona fide Pitney Bowes mark at all. It's an artifact. The forger took a Pitney Bowes imprint from another envelope, and then with a pin, punched holes in it along the lines. He then placed this over the envelope on which he wanted an imprint to appear, and patted some red ink down on the real Pitney Bowes imprint so that it would come through the little dots and leave an imprint on the forger's envelope." He called this the tattoo method, "... and a rank forgery."

On cross-examination Rhoden asked the expert, "Now, in order to have done this tattoo job, the forger had to have had an actual Pitney Bowes imprint made by a machine issued to someone in Las Vegas, Nevada, correct?"

The examiner responded, "Yes."

A representative from Pitney Bowes testified next. He was asked, "As an expert, can you tell us if this is a legitimate Pitney Bowes meter mark."

He said, "The quality is too poor to make a positive identification."

Rhoden then produced four envelopes that had been run through a Pitney Bowes machine by his secretary. She had tried four times and been successful four times, in duplicating the location and angle of the original envelope imprint. Then he asked, "... please take a look at the imprints on these envelopes dated today. Tell us, is the imprint on each of these envelopes in the same location and at the same angle as the Pitney Bowes imprint on the back of the will envelope?"

The expert answered, "Yes, they are all in the same location, and the same angle."

Rhoden followed up. Another expert "... testified that the imprint on the will envelope was too far down to have been made by a Pitney Bowes machine. He was wrong, wasn't he?"

"He was wrong."

Then Rhoden slammed the door. He said, an expert "... testified yesterday that he was positive that the Pitney Bowes imprint on the back of the will envelope was tattooed on there. As an expert on Pitney Bowes meter imprints, do you want to tell us the same thing he did?"

"Oh, no sir!"

The state investigator didn't attend all the trial sessions, so he may have missed the testimony of the Pitney Bowes expert. It's clear the will envelope could have been stamped by a Pitney Bowes machine.

The Attorney General's Office should have looked into the transparent violations of perjury and witness intimidation committed during the trial. They represented the citizens of Nevada, and a fair trial certainly was in the best interests of those citizens.

• • •

The various books I've read did very little to expand or investigate the Dummar affair. The authors essentially relied on information developed by others, much of it not totally accurate, and described the affair as "naive" or as a "hoax." The various pieces of information contained in the different volumes have not been pulled together. The authors assumed that since the will had been found to be fraudulent by the jury then, by inference, it was automatically assumed that Dummar's rescue of Hughes didn't occur. These are two different and distinct events and should be viewed as such.

The preliminary phase of this investigation was completed. Now was the time for an expanded investigative quest for the truth. I'd look into this case with an open mind, not lean-

ing one way or the other. I would let the facts develop and follow the investigative trails. Investigations can be unpredictable. You follow one trail and it leads you to some
answers, but it also may lead you to a dead end or to new
questions. You then follow that trail to where it leads, and so
on. The investigation could either exonerate or impeach
Melvin's story, or it could lead to a stone wall. Added to this is
the Howard Hughes legacy of complex, secret dealings, and
it's possible that the complete truth may never be known.

We can only speculate at this point as to how the old
man came to be on the dirt road. Sunset came at 5:15 P.M. in
late December. It began to grow darker, and the shadows
made it hard to see. Maybe the cold was more than the old
man had anticipated, and he had stayed longer than he
should have. He could barely see the ruts in the road.
Perhaps he stumbled and lost his balance. As he fell, he
caught himself, but his strength was gone. Maybe he cut his
head open and the blood ran down his neck. It wasn't coming in bursts, which would indicate arterial bleeding, but it
flowed steadily. It soaked his collar and spread to the shoulder of his shirt. He was tired and growing weaker. Of course,
it's entirely possible that the old man had been picked up by
someone and was robbed and assaulted and dumped on the
road. He was bleeding and exhausted—he was near death.

He may have lain in the dirt for some time, his head resting on his left arm. He lapsed in and out of consciousness.
The cold was seeping into his core. As he lay there, the
blood dried on his shirt and left ear. When Melvin lifted him
to his feet he described, "It was like lifting bones held
together with soft skin."

What caused the bleeding? Would the answer help identify the man picked up by Melvin in the desert? Additional

inquiry was required. Investigations are much like panning for gold. You slosh the sand and mud around in your pan, and if you're lucky you come up with a nugget or two.

A Web page entitled "Head Injuries" states, "Head injuries can be classified as either closed or penetrating... Common causes of head injury include accidents, falls, or physical assault... The signs and symptoms of a head injury may occur immediately or develop slowly over several hours... The following symptoms suggest a serious head injury: Fluid drainage from the nose, mouth, or ears (may be clear or bloody), loss of consciousness... Even if the skull is not fractured, the brain can bang against the inside of the skull and be damaged." Under the Internet heading "Healthwise" the following is found: "If bleeding from the ears or the nose is not caused by a cut or direct blow to the ears or nose, bloody drainage may indicate a fracture of the base of the skull..."

I spoke with an orthopedic surgeon. He informed me that bleeding from the ear can result from an acute ear infection or injury to the eardrum, but this bleeding would be very minimal, more of a slight oozing. He stated that a skull fracture would be the most likely cause of extensive bloody discharge from the ear. The bones of the skull are very strong, and it takes a substantial injury to the cranium to cause a depressed fracture. This type of fracture pushes the bone fragments inward, and the blood vessels in the meninges (the membrane that covers the brain) may be ruptured, resulting in the leakage of cerebrospinal fluid (the liquid that bathes the brain and spinal cord). This fluid often mixes with the blood from the ruptured blood vessels of the meninges and the leaking vessels from the cracked bone, and then can flow out through the nose or ears.

Did the desert vagrant fall while scouting the rugged terrain of Esmeralda County? Was he involved in an automobile accident and then walked away until he fell, unconscious, too weak to continue? Was he assaulted by someone and dumped? There is evidence that the bleeding could have been caused by blunt trauma severe enough to fracture the left skull inward. The injury caused the rupture of the meninges and blood vessels. Enough cerebral fluid mixed with blood leaked out of his left ear to cause a hand-sized stain on his shirt. We can also make some educated assumptions at this point. This degree of injury could not have occurred as a result of a simple fall. This catastrophic trauma could only occur from a fall off a fairly high place, such as a hill, or into a hole, such as a pit or mine shaft.

If the old-timer had been struck on the side of the head with a fist, it couldn't have caused the fracture. My training as a medic assigned to an aero-medical evacuation unit in the Air Force Reserve, taught me that the skull is very resilient and a reasonably reliable cover for the brain. It would take something more than a fist. Another possibility is that the man was involved in a vehicle crash. If he was driving alone, he could have driven off an embankment or rolled the vehicle. Since no one wore seat belts in 1967, he would have been thrown around inside the vehicle and could easily have bumped the side of his head hard enough to cause the injury. If he was in the vehicle with someone else driving, where was that person, and what happened to him?

The bleeding could have occurred at the site of the accident, where the man would have been incapacitated for some time with his head resting on his left shoulder, the blood covering his ear. When he came to and made his way down the road toward the highway, he may have collapsed again. Or the bleeding could have occurred as a delayed reaction and finally caused his loss of consciousness. Much of this, of course, is speculation on my part, but it should be thrown into the mix and maybe another piece of the puzzle will emerge.

It should be remembered that the man was found lying with his head away from the highway. This would be consistent with him walking away from the road, not towards it. Or it shows he was thrown out of a vehicle like a sack of garbage. If he drove, the road is very rough, and he must have had reservations about driving in the dark under those conditions. He may have parked his car off the highway and then got out to walk the road. He might have become disoriented or fallen in the dark.

I was certain that the vagrant had been a victim of an accident until I reread the Hughes autopsy report performed by Dr. Jack Titus, chairman of the Department of Pathology at Baylor College of Medicine. His findings necessitated a reevaluation of my theory of a skull fracture.

Titus reported that Hughes had suffered from kidney disease for ten years or longer. He also stated that there was a nodule, a small lump, on the left side of Hughes's head. He stated that the nodule was above the left ear. He later testified that this nodule had existed for five to ten years, and "It was slow growing, and would not have hurt him. It takes very little to traumatize because it sticks up and bleeds very easily. Combing his hair could have made it bleed. It was located in the left parietal scalp. That's over the left ear."

This revelation provides the reason for the presence of the bloodstain on the man's shirt. We can hypothesize that if the man was Hughes, he had brushed up against something with the left side of his head, which resulted in bleeding from the nodule. Or, he banged it on something or fell and hit the left side of his head on the road. Lastly, he may have been struck on the left side of the head by a fist.

The bleeding would have been fairly serious and could easily have soaked his shirt. Hughes, who lived a totally sedentary lifestyle for long periods of time, would have had leg muscles that were partially atrophied from disuse, and he would have had little endurance. His aides carried him on a stretcher up and down the nine floors of stairs at the Desert Inn because he was too weak to walk them himself. His weakness, the cold, and his bleeding could easily have drained what strength he had.

Dr. Norman Crane, Hughes's personal physician, testified in the trial, when he was asked, "Is it not proper medical practice for a doctor to keep a record of every injection he administers?"

"Yes, but years ago Mr. Hughes requested that I not keep any records."

"Did you examine Mr. Hughes?"

"Mr. Hughes would not allow the type of physical examination usually performed on patients."

Hughes's personal physician, who had no other patients, and who was very well compensated, didn't examine his lordly patient and kept no records. All he did was keep Hughes stoked with drugs. Hughes was deteriorating, but his doctor did nothing to help him. There would be no medical record of Hughes bleeding and collapsing in the desert.

During the probate trial, one of Hughes's personal aides, Howard Eckersley was asked, "Around 1968, did Mr. Hughes have any blood transfusions?"

Eckersley answered, "Yes, He was quite sick at that time."

Blood transfusions are usually given because of a significant loss of blood volume. Sometimes they are administered for kidney dysfunction. A loss of ten percent of blood volume can cause symptoms of shock. When volunteers give blood, one unit (one pint) is drawn. This loss of blood seldom produces shock symptoms, so we can infer that the man lost more than one pint. Could it be that if the man was Hughes, he had lost blood from the bleeding nodule on his head and had received the transfusions shortly after December 29, 1967 when Melvin picked him up? This could have occurred during the first few days of January 1968.

On March 1, 1976, one of Hughes's personal physicians reinforced my bleeding theory when he said that Hughes tried to get out of his bed on his own while living in Acapulco and fell. He hit something with his head, and it caused the nodule on his head to bleed profusely.

Melvin said he had seen no signs of trauma to the man's head and assumed that the bleeding was from the ear. He had no way of knowing about Hughes's nodule or bleeding potential. The nodule would have been covered by the man's shoulder length hair, and Melvin wouldn't have seen it. Is this just a coincidence, or is it evidence that the man was Hughes?

I wondered what position the old man's head had been in when he bled onto his shoulder. Was his head upright, or was it resting on his left shoulder? I am no scientist, but to answer the question in my own mind, I performed an experiment sometime after meeting with Melvin. I placed a cotton shirt around a wig dummy and expelled blood from a syringe just above the ear area. When the liquid was expelled in front of the ear, it ran down the neck to the collar of the shirt then continued down to the chest. When the blood was released behind the ear, it ran behind the shoulder to the back. Very little blood soaked the top of the shoulder. This result led me to presume that the man had his head lying on his shoulder, probably with the left arm extended, while bleeding onto the shirt. This means the man was lying down when much of the bleeding occurred.

My research shows the low temperature on December 29, 1967, was thirty-six degrees. It had only been six degrees warmer during the heat of day. There was no record of wind. The fact that the blood on the man's shoulder and ear was dried when Melvin picked him up is consistent with him being in the area for some time.

If Hughes needed a transfusion because of his "profuse" bleeding from his nodule, he would have lost more than ten percent of his blood volume. The body has ten pints of blood—this means he lost more than one pint. It could have been two, possibly more. I performed another experiment in an effort to determine how long Hughes may have lain in the road. Again, I'm no scientist, and my results couldn't be testified to by me. But the results give a good indication of time.

I took a pint of blood and let it drip from the container onto the shoulder of a shirt on a dummy positioned face down. It took approximately sixty minutes to empty the pint container a steady drop at a time. The blood soaked the shoulder, part of the collar, and slightly down the sleeve. But most of the blood ran off the shirt onto the table. In the case of the old man, most of the blood would have run off into the dirt.

We can presume that he lost one pint of blood or more. Otherwise, why would he need a transfusion? Losing one pint would have taken somewhere around sixty minutes before the bleeding stopped and the drying process began.

It would take about fifteen to twenty minutes for the blood to dry.

We can logically assume that the man lay in the road for at least one hour. After the bleeding stopped, it took another fifteen minutes to dry, so he would have been on the road helplessly face down for at least one hour and fifteen minutes.

If Melvin picked him up as late as 11:00 P.M., the man couldn't have started bleeding after 9:45 P.M. If Melvin picked him up at 9:00 P.M., he couldn't have started bleeding after 7:45 P.M. How long he was on the road before his bleeding began can't be known. I can't imagine Hughes trying to walk Howard's Road in the dark. What would he expect to see in the blackness?

One part of Melvin's story that never made sense to me was why would Hughes bequeath one-sixteenth of his vast estate to a man who merely gave him a ride to Las Vegas? It doesn't compute. But if Melvin had rescued Hughes from certain death from hypothermia and blood loss, then it makes complete sense.

As a medic in an aero-medical evacuation squadron in the Air Force Reserve, I was taught that hypothermia is a serious drop in core temperature. When the environmental temperature drops to fifty degrees or lower, a slightly covered body begins to lose heat. There is a much higher risk for the elderly because they can gradually lose sensitivity to lower temperatures and not be aware of the cold. If the body temperature drops to ninety-five degrees, severe shivering sets in, and drowsiness and disorientation overcome the victim. Speech becomes slurred and cognitive reasoning is impaired. When the body temperature drops to ninety degrees or lower, the muscles become rigid; pulse and respiration slow and the eyes glaze over. As the body temperature drops, unconsciousness or death can result. Loss of blood would compound these symptoms.

The rescued man certainly had most of these symptoms. He wasn't far from death. Hughes had been close to death before. He had been in numerous airplane crashes. He knew what facing death was like. He would have known he was dying, lying there in the road, helpless and lapsing in and out of consciousness. When he was rescued, he would have responded the way he always did. He would have assuredly rewarded his rescuer with money.

- 7 -

The Will

Two and a half decades after the probate trial, the handwriting expertise for the contestants is frequently highlighted as exemplary forensic work. The Dummar affair is often cited as one of the hallmark cases for forensic handwriting analysis. This is pure propaganda and complete nonsense.

The Las Vegas jury found the will to be illegitimate. Much of the evidence was based on handwriting testimony. A handwriting expert reviewed the will at the request of the Mormon Church before it was filed with the court in Las Vegas, and issued a preliminary opinion that the will was genuine. An autograph expert from New York City declared the Hughes signature on the will "... is indeed genuine... The signature looks exactly like Hughes's, and I think it would be exceedingly difficult to forge all aspects of that signature." Before the trial, two handwriting analysts hired by ABC News stated that they were certain the will was written by Hughes. During the trial, several nationally recognized American experts testified that they found the will to be fraudulent. Other foreign experts, highly recognized in their countries, said the will was written by Hughes. The focus of the trial seemed to be on the presentation of the case with an emphasis on handwriting experts, but this evidence turned out to be inconclusive. Because of this incongruity, I felt I needed to take a fresh approach at analyzing the will.

Was the Mormon Will legitimate, or was it some cheap attempt at fraud? After careful analysis of the probate trial testimony by those closest to Hughes, his personal aides, I have identified eight undeniable prerequisite elements of Howard Hughes's true will. Seven of these elements were universally agreed to in the aides's testimony. The elements are:

- The will was holographic (handwritten by the signer).
- It was written on yellow lined paper.
- The key people and aides were not listed by name, but by job description.
- A trusted person, unknown to the aides, held the will.
- The will had been in existence prior to 1970.
- As late as two weeks prior to Hughes's death in 1976, Hughes said he had a holographic will.
- Only Hughes had seen the will.
- The will would be sloppily prepared and filled with attentional errors.

All of the aides testified about a will described to them by Howard Hughes. They testified under oath as follows:

In 1974, Hughes told his aide, John Holmes, "Don't worry. I've got the holographic will that I just told you about." Holmes added, "He told me again that he had written it on a piece of yellow paper that had lines."

Chuck Waldron stated that in 1975, "… Well, we knew that somebody was holding a holographic will for Mr. Hughes. But we didn't know who. And we had to find out."

Later, during the probate trial, Waldron was asked, "Mr. Waldron, is it possible that Hughes could have written a will and gotten it out of his quarters without the aides knowing about it? Say, through a doctor acting as a courier?"

He answered, "Yes, that could happen."

George Francom testified that in 1975, while living with Hughes in the Bahamas, Hughes told him that he had written a holographic will. Francom was asked, "Did you ask him where it was?"

He responded, "Oh, yes. He said it was his business and nobody else's. He said, 'Do you think I'm going to tell you where it was?' We tried to assist him by getting him to tell us. But he just said, 'Don't bother looking for it, you're not going to find it.' We told him we didn't know when he had written it."

James Rickard stated that in 1972, "He (Hughes) said he had written a will… He said it many times, constantly."

Howard Eckersley received a memo from Hughes in 1972. It read as follows: "… I have had in existence for some time a holographic will covering the principle features of the points of substance set forth herein. It was carefully written seated at my desk, and complying to all the rules governing such a will… You as well as other members of my staff were identified by description rather than by name…"

During the trial, Eckersley was asked, "When was the last time Mr. Hughes told you he had prepared a handwritten will?"

He answered, "About a month before he died… Mr. Hughes said it was in a safe place. He said that nobody had seen his will except himself. He said something like, 'I gave it to someone I can trust to hold it for me.' He said he provided for us not by describing us by our names, but by general category or position... He said that whoever was holding it was not a guy who would betray a trust..."

Levar Myler, another of Hughes's personal aides, swore in a deposition that, beginning in 1970, Hughes talked about having a holographic will. He continued to mention the will up until two weeks prior to his death. He said Hughes warned, "Don't bother to look for it. You're never going to find it. It's safe. I've given it to somebody I can trust."

Evidence was presented during the trial proving that Hughes had chronic kidney disease. Therefore, his writing would have been adversely affected. His handwritten memos were filled with flaws during his latter years.

During the trial, a neurologist was asked, "Now, doctor, surely you cannot say, by looking at the will, that there are any indications that the writer of it had a kidney disorder?"

The physician smiled confidently. "Oh yes, I can! I detected things in the will, such as deletion of letters, faulty punctuation, oversimplification of thoughts, simple sentences, all consistent with the effect on the brain of renal failure. One example is leaving the *h* out of the word *children*. It's the type of attentional error committed by someone suffering from kidney disorder. Not a spelling error. Capitalization mistakes, for example, in the word *My*, in the middle of a sentence indicates poor attention concentration. I have seen similar errors in the handwriting of patients with uremic poisoning. The kinds of mistakes in this will were similar to mistakes made by brain-damaged people... I asked several other neurologists who have uremic poisoning patients to see if their experiences agreed with mine, if they also felt that those errors were indicative of kidney failure. I received universal agreement that that was the case. You will notice that parts of the will are very carefully done. Other parts are sloppy."

It would be consistent to conclude that the authentic Hughes will would conform to these eight very specific elements. Furthermore, the date on the will, if it was authentic, was made during the time David O. McKay was presiding over the Mormon Church. The will also states Hughes was a resident of Las Vegas at the time of the writing. This certainly suggests it was prepared before McKay died in January of 1970. The will envelope was addressed to "... Mr. McKay..." I wondered why a forger would include McKay's name on the envelope unless it was written while McKay was alive.

Additional medical testimony was presented during the trial as an explanation as to why some of the words in the will were misspelled and why so many grammatical errors and overwritings were made. A medical doctor testified that "... the kidney is a filter to rid the body of waste products; it separates chemicals in the blood and excretes waste into the urine. Renal failure is the failure of the kidneys to perform their filtering function. Uremia is a state in which, because of the kidney's failure, there is a flushing back of the poisonous waste into the blood system thereby keeping the kidneys from performing their filtering function."

The doctor was asked, "... how long did the deceased have the kidney disease that took his life?"

"Eight or ten years. It could have been more, but it is not likely to have been less... Uremic poisoning affects a person's ability to write and to spell words he would ordinarily spell correctly; sometimes a patient cannot correctly spell his own name."

"Doctor, take a word such as children in the questioned will. Would a person suffering from this disorder write that word leaving out the *h*?"

"That is precisely the type of abnormality I would expect from a person suffering from uremic poisoning."

Another doctor testified, "A person may suffer from the effects of uremic poisoning one hour, and not the next, one day and not the next, one week and not the next, and this can go on for years."

There was no significant cross-examination of these experts.

Hughes's insiders were shocked that Noah Dietrich was named as executor of the Hughes estate. They argued that he would never be named because he and Hughes had had a bitter falling out in 1957. They used this as an argument that the will was a fraud. Dietrich responded to the detractors by stating, "There's no question. It's his handwriting, and it's his signature. It's not just similar, it's the real thing." When Noah Dietrich was asked why he was named as the executor of the estate, he responded, "I knew more than anyone about his businesses, and he trusted me. He respected my ability and integrity."

During the trial, Rhoden asked Nadine Henley (Hughes's secretary) if she thought the Mormon Will was legitimate. She responded, "I would not!"

"Why not, ma'am?"

"Because I know this Mormon Will is a forgery."

She was asked to explain. "Please tell these jurors how you know that, Miss Henley."

She answered condescendingly, "Mr. Hughes was very well versed in the English language and its proper usage. He was very knowledgeable about punctuation and sentence structure. He would pick up mistakes on me, and I was an English major. He was a perfect speller, and it would bother him if he found that a secretary had misspelled a word. He could always catch me. He was meticulous. A perfectionist. He would argue with me over whether a word had a hyphen in it or not. He could not possibly have written those three pages."

In this material statement, Ms. Henley committed perjury. One of Hughes's own memos debunks her assertion. The will is indeed, replete with errors. These problems have been cited as proof that Hughes couldn't have written it. Many have said Hughes was a good speller, but a memo written by Hughes to Robert Maheu, his Chief of Las Vegas operations on December 4, 1966, indicates that Hughes was by no means perfect in spelling and composition. The memo states, "I have been notorious through the years for conducting all my business orally, usually by telephone. I am sure you have heard of this characteristic. When I started sending long hand written notes, my people protested long and loud. They wanted to retype my messages at least, and correct mistakes in composition and spelling, ect [sic] I said no, there was not time, and that I would ask you to return the messages so they would not get out of my hands in that condition."

A review of many of Hughes's memos found him to chronically misspell words. In the interest of brevity, I have only listed misspelled words I have culled from these few memos and not the entire text of the memoranda:

manafest

dont (used many times)

viscious

Humphries
wasnt
wouldnt
consistant
becide
competant
couldnt
practised

If I had access to additional memos, I'm sure there would be many more examples, possibly some of the exact misspellings as were written in the will.

Among the many wills submitted to the court was one typewritten document filed in Las Vegas. It provided one half of Hughes's estate to various charitable organizations and to "my tried and true friends" Frank William Gay, Chester Davis, and Nadine Henley. It also provided one half of the estate to Hughes's various relatives. The will was signed on March 8, 1976, and witnessed by three individuals.

A careful dissection of this particular will clearly debunks the document. This is the case with all the other typewritten wills that were submitted as well. First, my research shows Hughes would never have named his relatives, with the exception of his aunt and cousin William Lummis, as inheritors.

In 1947, Nadine Henley, whom Hughes treated like a sister, stated that she typed a will for Hughes that he never signed. This document was kept in a safe deposit box in Hollywood, California until 1974, when she moved it to Hughes's corporate headquarters in California. Hughes had no respect for his relatives in Texas. In a copy of his unsigned will he states, "I have intentionally omitted making provisions for all my heirs who are not specifically mentioned herein (William Lummis and his mother were named). I hereby generally and specifically disinherit each, any, and all persons whomever claiming to be or who may lawfully be determined to be my heirs at law, except such as are mentioned in this will." The original unsigned will has never surfaced.

Secondly, the date of this typewritten will was the time period that Hughes was in Acapulco, Mexico. He was in a completely weakened state, only one month prior to his death. The witnesses to the will couldn't have seen Hughes sign the document, as he was totally isolated from everyone except his closest aides. Thirdly, Hughes had said only he had seen the will. Fourthly, in this will, names of his key people were spelled out. This is not what he told his aides. They were to be listed by job description. Fifthly, this will was not a holographic will, which Hughes had stressed again and again that he had prepared by his own hand.

The only will adjudicated by the courts was the Mormon Will. It named Melvin DuMar [sic] of Gabbs, Nevada, among others, as an inheritor. This will, at the exclusion of all others, must be a major focus of this investigation.

I wondered why the proponents used foreign handwriting experts to authenticate the will. My research has determined that the team searched for American handwriting experts, but found many of them to be too expensive, unqualified, or intimidated by the threat of blacklisting in the United States. The expert used by the Mormon Church wasn't available because of prior commitments. This left the proponents in a bind. Rhoden told Marvin Mitchelson, "I need a panel of the most competent, prestigious handwriting experts in the world."

Mitchelson answered, "I'll go to Europe and get a panel."

The pivotal question that must be answered in my investigation is, did Howard Hughes leave the Desert Inn? If he did, why was he found in the desert in the middle of nowhere? Jim Dilworth, the lead attorney for the opposition to the will, stated after the trial, "It boiled down, really, to whether you believed Dummar's story about finding Hughes in the desert like that."

The jury agreed with this statement, as do I. Evidence that Hughes had disappeared and was in the Tonopah area at the right time period is the one essential key to corroborating Melvin's story about picking up Hughes. If this portion of his testimony can be corroborated, then he was telling the truth.

An inexplicable factor that casts doubt on the Mormon Will is the complete rejection of the will by Hughes's personal aides. They all testified that they believed the will to be a forgery, but I believe there is an explanation. That is, they felt secure with a sure thing. In other words, they had very good salaries. They had received bonuses and promises of lifelong consulting fees. They felt their jobs were safe. Bill Gay controlled Summa Corporation, and they believed this would not change over time. They didn't want to take any chances on an unknown will; besides they weren't the type of people to take chances. They were secure with what they had.

A template as to how Hughes handled a previously prepared will is enlightening. In 1938, Hughes wrote a letter to a bank. Part of the letter stated, "In the event of my death or disappearance, you are hereby instructed to take possession of these documents and open first the envelope containing the letter of instructions, being envelope No. 1, and to hold unopened the envelope containing the will, being Envelope

No, 2, in accordance with the instructions contained in Envelope No. 1." These early instructions are strikingly similar to those given by Hughes in 1972 when he turned over the care of the will to Forsythe.

• • •

I sat in the Ogden, Utah court reception area waiting to be escorted into the judge's chambers. The rain outside was coming in torrents. I could see the drops splashing off the asphalt road through the rain-splattered window. The day was gray and dark, and I hadn't slept well the night before. I just wanted to curl up in some warm place and sleep. I had just closed my eyes and leaned back in the hard wooden chair when I was interrupted back to reality.

The receptionist escorted me to Judge Roger Dutson's office. The office was small, not anything like the federal judges' chambers I had been in. Ten of Dutson's offices would have fit inside a federal judge's chambers. This office was much more utilitarian, kept by someone accustomed to turning out work. Much more blue collar as opposed to the ivory-tower approach of federal judges. I suppose it could be argued that federal judges handle more complex matters, and their decisions affect more people, but why do they need an extremely expensive upscale suite to do their work? I have nothing against federal judges. They are usually very competent and honest. There was a judge who referred to me as his favorite Norwegian FBI agent because he was of Norwegian heritage and wanted an authentic Norwegian name for his cottage in the woods. I was able to assist him because I speak Norwegian. Other federal judges have been equally gracious.

Judge Dutson had been Melvin's attorney during the trial. He had been elected judge many years later. He was seated behind his desk when I entered his office, but he walked around the desk and seated himself in a chair next to me. This was a thoughtful gesture implying that we were now equals. I handed him a waiver signed by Melvin that morning. It dissolved the attorney-client privilege between the two and allowed Dutson to speak freely. When I first interviewed Judge Dutson, he was somewhat reluctant to open up completely, probably because speaking out of school about a client was alien to him. He explained that Melvin had led a hard life. During the interview he stated over and over again, "All he had to do was tell the truth. Melvin has a personality hang-up about the truth. When a problem comes up he will not admit the problem. It's like pulling teeth."

The judge explained that Melvin might have unconsciously learned this behavior as a child. This fear of being caught causes him to squirm and tell other stories to cover the first one. He said, "Melvin told the whole world that he hadn't seen the will before it came to light. This was the one thing that hurt us the most."

Melvin thought he was being smart by denying the will, but in the end it was the lie that hung over the trial like a storm cloud and threw a shadow on everything else. The judge added, "He thought people would think he was involved in the forgery if he admitted that the will had been delivered to him, but if he would have admitted it, it wouldn't have tainted the trial nearly as much as the lie he told. If he had told the truth, we could have overcome that problem."

Judge Dutson explained that he had represented Melvin in his various criminal charges when he was a practicing attorney and had been successful in getting the charges dismissed. Melvin asked him for help when the will came to light and when the pressures finally overwhelmed him. Dutson and his firm agreed to represent him for a ten percent contingency fee. This fee is very low by contingency standards, but they felt the total inheritance was significant enough to offset the low fee. He and his firm spent a great deal of their own money on the trial. Dutson lived full time in Las Vegas during the trial period. I asked the judge, "After all the headaches and problems of the trial, what do you think about the will?"

He responded without hesitation. "I believe Melvin picked up Howard Hughes in the desert, and I believe the will was probably written by Howard Hughes. I read hundreds of Hughes's memos, and Melvin couldn't have written that will. There were too many unique characteristics to Hughes's writing, misspellings, and overwritings. These characteristics were clear in the will."

He mentioned an incident during the trial where LeVane Forsythe had received a telephone call threatening him if he testified. My review of the record shows that on March 7, 1977, attorney Harold Rhoden listened to a tape of the call that had been recorded by Forsythe. The transcript shows an anonymous caller asked, "Are you LeVane Forsythe?"

Forsythe answered, "Yeah."

The caller continued, "I'm gonna tell you this only once. If you get on that witness stand in Las Vegas and shoot off your mouth about any deliveries you made to the capital, you ain't gonna get out of Las Vegas alive!"

Judge Dutson explained that Forsythe wouldn't testify because of the threat, and they had to rely on reading Forsythe's sworn deposition into the record. The judge believes that this testimony would have been much more effective had Forsythe testified in person. Realistically, a boring reading of a statement into the record doesn't have the same impact as the testimony of a live witness. The jury can't get the flavor of the witness.

Tragically, Harold Rhoden and his family were all killed in a private airplane crash some years ago. He had purchased an airplane, not long after the probate trial to pursue his love of flying. It was my hope that he would be able to fill me in on many details of the pre-trial investigation, but events made that impossible.

I was able to find Rhoden's former secretary, Linda Acaldo. She is a small woman with the heart of a lion. She moved to Las Vegas during the probate trial and assisted Rhoden during the complete proceedings. She told me she was so disgusted with the outcome of the trial, and what she considered a poor performance by Rhoden, that she became convinced she could have done a better job. As a result, she went on to college and law school and became an assistant district attorney. I contacted her, and she consented to meet me at a resort near her home. Apparently her experience as an assistant D.A. made her wary of strangers, as she wanted to meet in a public place. We sat and talked at an outside table in the late afternoon. The sun was setting, and I could feel the mountain chill seeping into my bones as the sun disappeared behind the pines.

She recalled with a sneer, "Hal Rhoden was a one-man show. He didn't give anyone else a chance, and he wouldn't listen to anyone. We could have won that trial, but the jury so disliked his style that they had no empathy for him or our case."

Linda Acaldo, was Marvin Mitchelson's secretary. She was loaned to Harold Rhoden for the trial. She attended strategy sessions, sat in on much of the trial, and did a great deal of research on the case. She informed me she left Las Vegas in a disgusted rush after the trial. She stated that she truly believes that the American handwriting experts were intimidated by the threat of being expelled and blacklisted by their peers if they testified in opposition to the president of the organization. Those who testified against the will, along with their president, strengthened their position within the national organization.

"What can you tell me about the trial that sticks out in your mind after all these years?" I asked hopefully.

She smiled slightly, as if she were holding some hidden secret. "I reviewed everything for Hal. If there was any analysis of documents or evidence, I did it. I came across a memo from Hughes in which he stated that he had a secret messenger who lived in L.A. LeVane Forsythe lived in L.A. at the time. I'm sure the memo referred to him."

I have located this particular memo. In part it states, "... I will send a most trusted envoy to him from Los Angeles—a man with whom I would trust my life and this envoy will bring the message to me unopened." I wondered, did this mean the envoy would personally deliver the message to Hughes or to one of the aides?

Then, as if saving the best for last, Acaldo released her most important revelation. She said she had reviewed records of the aides's suites. She wanted to place these records before the jury, but with some contempt in her voice, she said, "Hal said we didn't need the evidence as we would win without it, and it would be too difficult to get a custodian of records from the Desert Inn to properly enter the evidence in trial." Linda vehemently disagreed with this decision, but she had no say in the matter. "I was only a sec-retary," she emphasized sarcastically.

She told me she had reviewed Desert Inn records for all of the aides's rooms for the period prior to the end of December of 1967, through early 1968. Unfortunately, these records were discarded after the trial. These records showed numerous daily outgoing phone calls from all of the suites, as well as room service meals that were delivered daily to the aides in their suites. The records showed that there was substantial activity in the suites until the twenty-seventh. She explained, "Beginning on December 27th and through December 30, 1967, there were no outgoing phone charges and no room service meals charged to the aides's suites. On December thirty-first, the charges started again. Those aides were not in their suites for that four-day period. Where were they?"

I responded somewhat facetiously, "Maybe they were with Howard Hughes, away from the Desert Inn!"

She smiled slyly. "I can't believe we didn't use that evidence. It proved the aides weren't at the Desert Inn during the pertinent period."

As I contemplated this new evidence, it became clear that the aides may have been with Hughes, or they may have gone home for a little family time between Christmas and New Year's Eve because they knew Hughes would be gone. Unfortunately, the true answer is in the wind.

Melvin's wife, Bonnie, has strenuously denied forging the will. I asked her if she had any part in forging the document. She laughed and said, "No." She said her life had been ruined by the will, and she resents Hughes a great deal. Then she forcefully told me, "When I die, the first thing I'm gonna do is look up Howard Hughes and make things so miserable for him that he will wish he was alive."

Some months after I initiated this inquiry, I learned that

Howard Eckersley, a once handsome man who had been one of Hughes aides, had passed away in late 2003 after a long illness. I learned that his memory had faded to nearly nothing. His last years were difficult as he barely recognized his own family. Time has taken its toll on many potential witnesses, and now, he would have to be counted among that expanding group.

I was particularly focused on Eckersley's possible complicity in secretly moving Hughes out of the Desert Inn. He was on duty on December 26, 1967, when Hughes may have left the hotel. Unfortunately, his eyewitness account is impossible now.

I was able to locate his son, and he told me that his father had never mentioned sneaking Hughes out of the Desert Inn, but he did take credit for spiriting Hughes from his hotel under cover of darkness in London when Hughes piloted his last flight in 1973. This was interesting as it's a fact that Eckersley was involved in slipping Hughes into the Desert Inn in 1966. He was also involved in moving Hughes, undetected, out of the Desert Inn in 1970, and he had admitted moving Hughes surreptitiously in and out of his London hotel when Hughes flew for the last time. It certainly seems logical that he had expertise in moving the boss without being detected. Getting Hughes out of the Desert Inn would have been a relatively easy procedure and part of the pattern of escape participated in by Eckersley.

• • •

When I first began this inquiry, I did so as a personal challenge, but as I dug deeper into the evidentiary compost pile, my perspective changed. Now the investigation has become a matter of justice. I've always been troubled by the denial of justice. The biggest, richest, and strongest among us naturally prevail. That's why we have laws, to level the field, to give the weak a voice, to make things equal. In this case that did not happen, as the trial process failed and justice was denied.

I recall a case I investigated as an agent some years ago. A man would seduce older women and convince them to invest in his racehorse. He told them all kinds of stories about his winning record. He had photos of the horse in the winner's circle with him standing next to it. He told the women he cared so much for them that he wanted them to profit along with him. The only problem was that he didn't own a horse, and he sold shares in the same nonexistent horse over and over. He robbed these widows of everything they had. He left them destitute. This wasn't the biggest case I ever worked, but it was one of the most satisfying. When I arrested the man after kicking the coward's door in, I felt a sense of victory. These ordinary, nameless widows finally received justice.

"I can't believe you guys are so naive about your enemy! You're talking about a ton of money here. Don't you think those damn people will do anything to get it?" Forsythe took another swallow of beer and looked around the table. He continued his soliloquy. "You guys might know the law, but you don't know how far these lowlifes will go. They've got a spy on your team, and they'll try to buy the jury if they can!"

The lawyers glanced at Forsythe, but only for a moment. Then they continued eating their meals. Lawyers don't like to hear about corruption in the court system. After all, it's their system. The law is their life. To think that the system has somehow been corrupted makes them very uneasy. The undeniable fact is that the courts deal with crooks. Why would a hardened criminal be willing to go down and be convicted if he has an option to control the outcome of the trial? In civil cases there are no crooks, per se, but when large sums of money are involved, the same motivation exists to control the outcome.

After the verdict came down in the probate trial, one of the proponent attorneys was pulled to the side and told by Forsythe that a member of the jury might have been compromised. The lawyer doesn't know how Forsythe obtained this information. Later, it was rumored that a juror had markers (gambling debts) forgiven at several casinos. It was also rumored that he was given a suite in the penthouse of the Desert Inn Hotel as a reward after the trial.

Judge Dutson, the lead attorney for the Dummar team, believes the contestants bought the opinions of the handwriting experts by paying extravagant fees. He said that one of the famous American experts demanded ten thousand dollars to come to Las Vegas to view the will and fifty thousand dollars to testify. He doesn't believe that the opposition had a mole, nor that the jury was fixed, but he left this portion of the inquiry up to one of his partners and, therefore, he couldn't be totally sure.

During long trials, the debris of rumors and suspicion spin around in the wind. Trying to put your finger on the debris is a problem. How do you track down the rumor without appearing to step on the system's constitutional guarantees? There was some investigation after the trial by a proponent attorney, but it came to nothing.

I hate loose ends! Was there evidence of jury tampering? The jury consisted of a bank loan officer, a police department administrative analyst, a customer service agent for an airline, a seventy-two-year-old grandmother, a housewife, an advertising executive, a schoolteacher, and a casino employee.

Lowell M. Sylvester was a member of the jury. He is the

only surviving member I was able to locate. When I contacted him, he told me, "We found the will to be phony because we didn't believe Hughes ever left the Desert Inn Hotel. There was a lot of evidence that he never left the building."

I was familiar with the trial testimony as a result of my research into the probate trial, so I inquired, "What about the cowboy who saw him near American Flat, and the guy who said he saw him in Tonopah at the Mizpah Hotel?"

Sylvester thought for a moment. "I don't remember hearing that," he responded.

I asked him about Dr. Ford's testimony where he described a conversation in which Kay Glenn told Ford that Hughes was lost in the desert and was picked up by someone. Sylvester couldn't recall that testimony either. He couldn't recall the aides testifying about Hughes telling them about the holographic will, and he couldn't remember anyone saying it was possible to leave the Desert Inn penthouse by way of a fire stairwell. Even accounting for the passage of time, the evidence apparently was not prominent in his memory. Was this a function of poor case presentation, lost memory, or clever manipulation by outside forces?

The jury had been wearied by eight months of testimony. Imagine sitting hour after hour, day after day, listening to the droning of handwriting experts, and the cross-examinations regarding pen lifts, overwrites, and letter characteristics. Add to this, the constant turbulence of objections and legal wrangling by the attorneys. A normal person can't be expected to recall all of the evidence. A normal person becomes stupefied and the eyes glaze over, and by the end of the trial, memories are blurred. Clearly, during the marathon trial, the evidence of the eyewitnesses attesting that Hughes left the Desert Inn was not stressed enough by the proponents.

Sylvester continued, "The handwriting testimony was just confusing. You had the European experts saying there was no doubt that Hughes wrote the will, then you had the American experts say it was a forgery. We came to the conclusion that the handwriting evidence was too contradictory."

I asked him about the process of choosing a foreman of the jury, and he explained, "One of the jurors took very extensive notes during the trial, and then he would go home and type them up at night. He showed us the notes. We were very impressed with the logical, precise way they were laid out. Once we saw his notes, he asked to be elected foreman, so we chose him."

Detailed notes would be essential during the deliberation process. Sylvester and the others logically relied on the best notes after eight months of trial. It's very interesting that the man selected as the foreman took the trouble to type his notes every night. This is unheard of. Why would that be necessary if he had handwritten notes? Could it be that he hoped to sell the notes after the trial, or was he trying to impress the other jurors so they would rely on his notes and not their own? Or, could the notes have been prepared by someone else? This could be easily done. Someone with good typing skills, such as a secretary, could have typed the notes. There would be a great deal of testimony and many details that would need to be covered. The typed notes could have been delivered to the foreman at night and he would bring them to court the next morning. Once the jurors relied on the foreman's notes, they would naturally minimize their own note taking.

It appears the evidence presented showing Hughes had left the Desert Inn and was seen in Tonopah was lost in the foreman's typewritten notes. Many other details could also have been deleted or glossed over.

I asked, "Was the jury united against the will from the beginning?"

"It's so long ago, but I think we took a preliminary vote, and the jury was basically evenly divided for and against the will. As we reviewed the notes and discussed the evidence, we came to believe that the will was a fraud."

Sylvester had never heard the allegation that a member of the jury was paid off. He also said that he had never heard of the foreman having his gambling markers erased, or that he was "comped" at the Desert Inn after the trial.

A television reporter interviewed Richard Wright (believed to be deceased), the jury foreman, a short time after the probate trial concluded in 1978. The reporter heard allegations of bribery. He asked Wright what he understood the allegations against him were. He responded, "Allegations that thirty-seven thousand dollars was spread between myself and four other jurors. I don't know why I was singled out except that I was the foreman of the jury. And I was wined and dined at the Desert Inn, that I had a couple of bodyguards that took care of a couple of favors for me. Plus, a credit check was run on me and that I was deep in debt and it was all taken care of."

The reporter responded, "That's a serious charge."

"Yes, it is."

"Do you have any gambling debts?"

"No."

"Did you come into some money?"

"No!"

"Were you wined and dined?"

"No."

This questioning of Wright was obviously a television sound bite and nothing more. The reporter had no evidence to confront Wright with and merely asked him questions that any accused person could easily deny. Wright could have been telling the truth when he was asked if he had any gambling debts. If they had been written off by the casino, he wouldn't have had any debt. Also, when he said he didn't receive any money, he might have been telling the truth. The write-off would have been a paper transaction, and no money may have changed hands. If, at one time, there was evidence of jury bribery, it's long gone.

Now we have to dissect the subject of jury tampering. How is the approach of a juror made? It's like walking on hot coals. It's not possible to approach the entire jury. You have to be selective. It's like shooting ducks. You never shoot at the whole flock. You pick your target.

Each prospective juror is required to fill out a questionnaire. This provides information for the lawyers about that person. This assists the lawyers in determining whom they should select for the final jury pool. By obtaining a copy of these confidential questionnaires, a third party can easily determine, through additional background investigation, information that can be used in assessing a potential target for manipulation. Is the person strapped for money? Can he be blackmailed or threatened? Do we know someone who may know him, and who can make the approach? In 1977, the Las Vegas gaming community was a fairly small one. If a juror were a big gambler and had outstanding markers, it would be readily known.

Once it's been determined who the target is, the

approach is made. It can easily blow up because the target could go to the authorities. This is why juries are seldom tampered with. It's too dangerous. The consequences are too problematic. Judges are absolutely protective of their system and come down hard on this sort of tampering.

How can one juror influence a whole jury? In a criminal trial, one juror can cause a hung jury. I once had a case where the jury was eleven to one for conviction, but one man refused to discuss the evidence, turned his back on the others, and read the newspaper for five days during jury deliberations. After days of exasperation, the judge had to call a mistrial. A subsequent investigation of the juror showed he was a nut and not corrupt.

In a civil trial the bad juror has to be able to convert others to his position. This isn't an easy task. Convincing the others that the bad juror has the best trial notes might do it. Remember that the trial lasted eight months. Memories can be very short and confused, and reliance on notes would be vital.

Unfortunately, we'll probably never know. The passage of time has washed away evidence of jury tampering. There are no gaming credit records for that time period, and the room records of the Desert Inn are long gone. I was unable to find any other jurors. If the juror was given a suite at the Desert Inn, who had authority to provide this complimentary gift? One person who had the authority was Chester Davis.

• • •

"I was a reporter for a radio station and did some freelance work for a television station in Salt Lake. The Hughes probate trial held thousands of people spellbound for months, and I was very much involved in the press coverage." Ray Friess leaned back in his overstuffed chair as he recounted pleasant memories of the past. He went on to explain that a former close friend of Hughes, James Bryant, had informed Friess that Hughes had told him on one occasion that he admired the Mormon Church and wanted to leave some money to the church. Hughes also mentioned leaving money to other organizations he respected.

If Hughes wrote the Mormon Will, he had finally come to the realization that his vast wealth should be used for a greater purpose.

He had moved beyond his self-absorbed hedonism with his bequest of huge amounts of money to medical research, universities, orphans, the Boy Scouts, the Mormon Church, and finally, his rescuer.

"I understand there were all kinds of rumors about jury fixing after the trial. Are you aware of any of that?" I asked.

"Yes, LeVane Forsythe told me the jury was fixed. I think two other people mentioned it also, but I can't remember who they were.

Forsythe told me the jury foreman and three other jurors received thirty-seven thousand dollars in bribe money, and the foreman had gambling debts taken care of."

"Were you able to confirm any of this information?"

"No, it was very difficult to do. I called the foreman and spoke to him, but he denied it."

Friess interviewed several of Hughes's aides during the trial period. He called Kay Glenn, supervisor of the aides, and confronted him with the fact that Dr. Ford was going to testify that Glenn had told him about Hughes being out of the Desert Inn. Glenn erupted, "Holy shit, he can't do that! I'll call him! I've got to stop him!"

Freiss explained that Glenn was completely flustered by this news. In the emotion of the moment, Glenn stated that he had to stop this testimony as it would be devastating.

Friess explained that Glenn essentially admitted that the story was true, and it would ruin everything.

This information was hearsay and couldn't be introduced in court, but it should have been considered by reasonable people. Friess also said that he had received threatening phone calls during his period of investigative reporting. He was told to stop asking questions about the jury. Friess would only have been threatened if he was approaching sensitive information that could have caused serious repercussions to certain parties. Otherwise, why take the chance to make a threat to a reporter?

• • •

The contestants of the will used whatever legal means were available to them to gain an advantage in the trial. In a Reno, Nevada courtroom, before the probate trial began, Paul Freeze addressed the court. "... Your honor. Judge Hayes ought to be disqualified from trying this will contest whether he is biased or not. He ought to be disqualified because charges have been made that he is biased."

The argument focused on the point that Judge Hayes was a Mormon, and since the Church of Jesus Christ of Latter-day Saints was named in the will, he would have an inherent bias towards the authenticity of the will. On August 15, 1977, the Reno judge ruled on the motion. "If Judge Hayes continues to preside in this case, a cloud of unwarranted suspicion will hang over it. Therefore, Judge Hayes is hereby disqualified from acting further in this case."

On August 25, 1977, the Nevada Supreme Court reinstated Judge Hayes as the trial judge. They found there had been no basis for the bias allegation. It can be argued that attempting to disqualify a judge is a legitimate legal tactic, but the tactic was unsuccessful.

This move put Freeze in the awkward position with the judge. He was now forced to argue before Judge Hayes after besmirching his integrity. Freeze tried to overcome this difficulty by providing the court with a lengthy biography listing his history and evidence of his evenhandedness. I don't know if it's possible to kiss and make up after such an attack on the integrity of a judge.

An attorney who was on the proponent team told me that he believed the opponents had a mole inside their group. Every time they developed a new witness, the other side seemed to be aware of it. This may or may not be true. I'm not sure how helpful it would have been to the contestants. There is no evidence that this occurred, except for Forsythe's allegation.

• • •

Mell Stewart is a Utah country boy. He and I sat in his den, where the walls were covered with the stuffed heads of trophy elk, deer, and mountain goats. Apparently he is as good with a rifle as he was with a razor. Stewart obtained a barber's license in California and was cutting hair, minding his own business, when he received a call asking him to come to the Beverly Hills Hotel in 1957. He was asked to cut Howard Hughes's hair, and they became friends. Even when he moved his business to Utah, he was flown to California by Hughes to cut his hair. Over time, he did personal favors for Hughes and was asked to entertain businessmen for the Hughes Empire. When Hughes moved to Las Vegas, Stewart moved there with him. He had a suite in the Desert Inn Hotel and frequently ran errands for Hughes. One of his duties was to "... run all over town to get isopropyl alcohol. Hughes never washed with soap and water, but bathed himself in alcohol."

Stewart has little respect for many of the aides and related an incident that caused them great alarm. He said, "They had run out of bottled water, which they flew in from Maine. Hughes would only drink this Poland water. They were completely beside themselves, not knowing what to do. So I took some bottles and went to the bathroom next door and filled them with tap water. Problem solved."

Stewart described many of the aides as greedy crooks who stole whatever they could. They constantly offered him opportunities to enrich himself, but he responded, "My soul is not for sale, and you can't buy it." Stewart wasn't put on retainer after Hughes's death like the aides were, so he moved away and lived his own life. He said he didn't know anything about Hughes leaving the Desert Inn while he lived there.

James Rickard testified that he had worked for Hughes since 1953. He became a personal aide after Hughes left Las Vegas in 1970. He testified that in 1972, after leaving Vancouver with Hughes, "... we did destroy some of the Vancouver logs, yes."

Kay Glenn, the supervisor of the aides, and clearly the man who ran the show on the ninth floor, testified that he had started working for Hughes in 1950 as a stenographer. He said he didn't see Hughes face-to-face between 1966 and February 1976. He was asked, "What did you do with the logs after Mr. Hughes checked out of the Desert Inn?"

"I ordered them shredded and the remains burned." Glenn also ordered the logs to be destroyed after Hughes left Acapulco, Mexico in 1976. Glenn testified that he reported directly to Bill Gay. Investigation showed the aides destroyed the daily logs from the Desert Inn Hotel for the period of December 1967 through January 1968. Without the logs, it was almost impossible to determine the whereabouts of

Hughes on the pertinent days in question.

Why would the destruction of the logs be so vital? Many were destroyed in Vancouver; they were destroyed in Las Vegas; and they were destroyed in Mexico. Could it be that they were destroyed to cover up the fact that Hughes was out of the Desert Inn for a period of a few days in December 1967, and that Forsythe had met with Hughes in 1972 while in Vancouver, and because they would have shown the disregard and neglect shown to Hughes before he died?

Kay Glenn's life has slowed down. He lives in Salt Lake City now and minds his own business. He described his employment with Hughes as a "hell of a job while it lasted." He went on to say, "I know Maheu was livid when he learned we had slipped Mr. Hughes out of the Desert Inn in 1970. His security was so relaxed. I organized it, and they went down the stairs right under his nose." Glenn's contempt for Maheu was obvious even after all these years.

I asked, "If the security was so lax, why couldn't Hughes have left the Desert Inn another time while he stayed there?"

"I was in charge of the aides, and he never left the hotel."

"Were you there all the time?" I asked.

"No."

"What about the will? Do you think it was legitimate?"

"No, it was against his wishes. He wouldn't give his money to the church or some of the other groups. It was not his will."

He went on to stress, "I'm telling you, Howard Hughes never left the confines of his suite at the Desert Inn Hotel while he lived in Las Vegas! Since he didn't leave, he couldn't have been in the desert, and since he wasn't in the desert, Melvin Dummar couldn't have picked him up."

When he made this emphatic statement, I thought, what

about Dr. Ford's testimony? Did he testify falsely, or was Glenn lying?

The faithful aides who stuck to the party line and were good soldiers in protecting the interest of Hughes's key people were rewarded with lifetime "consulting" jobs. These consulting fees were nothing more than a means to keep them in line. Chuck Waldron testified he had received a consultant's position with Summa after Hughes's death. He continued as an executive assistant at the time of the trial. He was asked, "What do you do as an executive assistant? Do you supervise anyone?"

"No."

"Do you receive reports from anyone?"

"No."

"Exactly what do you do as an assistant?"

"I'm available to consult."

"With whom?"

"With anybody."

"About what?"

"Whatever he wants."

George Francom leaned back in his chair, his seventy-four-year-old legs resting on an ottoman. He seemed to be a contented man in spite of his poor health. He has a degenerative neurological disease that has struck his legs. They are wasting away, and he has lost much of his strength. Recently, while working in his yard, he had fallen into a prickly pear cactus. Luckily, the unintended acupuncture wasn't too serious, but he had cactus needles stuck all over his body. Because of the accident, he is much more careful and has cut back on his physical activity.

George Francom, one of the few aides who enjoys a good reputation, told me, "I was on the outside of the inside circle. I had been with Mr. Hughes for the longest time of all. I was with him in Tonopah when he was married. I wasn't invited into the room, but I was there. Later, when Bill Gay came on board, he hired the others, and they didn't trust me because I wasn't a team player. The others did things that I believed were wrong, and I didn't want any part of it. I kept to myself, and I was shunned because of it. They couldn't get rid of me because Mr. Hughes liked me, and they knew it. I didn't do as well financially as the others because I maintained my honesty and did my job. My family was more important to me than following the edicts of Bill Gay. The other aides met with Gay all the time. They talked to him on the phone and provided intelligence on everything and everyone. They were his eyes and ears. I kept my distance. He didn't like that either. He wanted to know everything."

He explained that Hughes's handlers convinced Hughes to go to Mexico because they told him that obtaining codeine was becoming more difficult in the United States, and they could get whatever they wanted in Mexico. Hughes's addiction was so severe at this point that he would do anything to relieve his suffering. Francom remembered several occasions where he saw Hughes with syringes sticking out of his arm. He had injected himself and then had fallen into a drug stupor. While in this state of addiction, his handlers got Hughes to sign all kinds of documents expanding their authority and approving their lifelong retainers.

When I asked Francom if he thought Hughes had explored mines near Tonopah, he responded, "No, I don't think he ever left the Desert Inn. Besides, he was very weak, and he couldn't walk very far."

"Why don't you think he left the Desert Inn?" I asked.

"Like I said, I never heard a word about it," he responded.

"Did you work twenty-four hours a day, seven days a week?"

"No, of course not. I had days off when I wasn't at the hotel."

"Did you have a suite at the hotel?"

"No. I had a house, but all the others had suites there."

I asked, "Is it possible that some of the others, along with Hughes, could have left the hotel by the fire stairwell without your knowledge?"

"Of course, it's possible. I can't say for absolutely sure that he didn't leave. If they did take him to Tonopah they would never have told me about it, especially if something had gone wrong."

Francom recounted a time on April 1, 1976, when Hughes seemed melancholy and lamented, "George, I suppose I should have been more like other men; I was not nearly as interested in people as I should have been. But I'm not a robot, as some have called me. I was merely consumed by my interest in science."

Francom explained that while the other aides received lifelong retainers after Hughes died, he was limited to three years. He received no special benefits after Hughes's death while the others reaped great rewards. Gay cut off Francom because he had a strong relationship with Hughes, and Francom passed messages to various people on the outside. He was later confronted by Gay for this unpardonable indiscretion and paid dearly for it with a substantial loss of income.

People close to this story have various theories on the legitimacy of the will. George Francom told me what he thought of the Mormon Will. He responded, "I think it was a fraud. I think Noah Dietrich and Melvin Dummar were in it together somehow. I don't have any facts, but I've always thought there was something there."

Francom expressed his theory about the will, but consideration should be given to the fact that Dietrich always denied knowing Melvin. Melvin also denied knowing Dietrich. Of course, they could have lied about that, as co-conspirators always do, but when Dietrich first heard the will read to him over the phone he exclaimed, "Hal, forget it! It's a hoax."

Harold Rhoden asked, "How do you know, Noah?"

He responded, "A newsman read it to me over the phone. It names the Spruce Goose, and Howard would never have used that name. And the spelling is childish. Don't waste your time."

If Dietrich and Melvin were in on the forgery together, why would Dietrich initially say the will was a hoax? Francom's theory doesn't add up.

Later, after having seen an actual copy of the will, Dietrich announced, "Hal, drop everything. Howard wrote it! I have it right here. An AP reporter just flew in from Las Vegas with a Xerox copy. It's Howard's handwriting! I'd know it anywhere!"

Linda Acaldo told me that she believed Melvin had picked up Hughes in the desert, but she had an interesting theory on the origin of the will. She agreed that Forsythe had delivered the will to Melvin, but she theorized that Melvin had copied much of it and included himself as an inheritor, and then disposed of the original. This theory surprised me as I thought she would have supported the will as having been written by Hughes. In response to her hypothesis, I asked her why Forsythe delivered the will to Melvin and not to the Mormon Church if Melvin wasn't named in the original will?

She explained, "Forsythe didn't want to be troubled by potential problems, and besides, he was directed by phone, to 'deliver this to Melvin Dummar of Gabbs, Nevada.'" She assumed that Melvin should have gotten the two thousand eight hundred dollars from the other envelope, but Forsythe took it instead. She also said that the Paper Mate ballpoint pens that Hughes used in 1968 were often passed out to various people as souvenirs after Hughes had used them. She assumed that Melvin might have gotten one somehow.

This theory is an interesting one, but it has holes. The authorities never tied Melvin's handwriting to the will, and Melvin having one of Hughes's pens is a stretch. The Paper Mate pens were used by Hughes in Las Vegas until November of 1970, when he left the country. The will wasn't delivered to Melvin until 1976. If he did happen to have one of the pens, he would have had to hold it for six years, and then pulled it out to forge a will after the original was delivered to him by Forsythe. How did Melvin know that Hughes used a Paper Mate exclusively during the pertinent time period? And what about the use of yellow lined paper? This evidence didn't come out until the trial. Forsythe had three envelopes given to him by Hughes. One said "mail this." One said "deliver this," and the third said "open this." The one labeled "open this" contained money. It was clearly meant for Forsythe and not Melvin.

Also, why did Forsythe ask Melvin, "Wouldn't it be something if you were in his will and got some money from the Hughes estate," if Melvin wasn't already named in the will? And, why would Melvin misspell his own last name in the will if he forged it?

James Rickard, the only surviving aide besides Francom,

as far as I'm aware, told me that he had joined Hughes's personal staff after he left Las Vegas. Rickard, a fragile, seemingly gentle man, told me that he knew nothing about the Hughes's mining operations. I asked him if he had heard any rumors about Hughes leaving the Desert Inn.

He responded, "There was always someone with him, but I don't know for sure. I don't think he did."

When I spoke with Robert Maheu, he told me that it was his belief that the will was "phony." He explained that he didn't believe that Hughes could have been out of the Desert Inn, and therefore, Dummar couldn't have picked him up. If Dummar didn't pick up Hughes, then he would never have been named in Hughes's will.

Maheu stated, "I was involved for the first time in year-end discussions with Hughes in late 1967. These discussions covered problems, taxes, and other matters. Once Hughes started off on a project, he didn't stop until it was resolved." Maheu said that he personally "... checked with the tax attorney..." regarding the matters that Hughes had wanted resolved. Maheu reiterated that Hughes "... never left his room..." while living in the Desert Inn.

I'm convinced that Maheu believes that the will is fraudulent and that Hughes could not have left the Desert Inn. However, a few points of fact must be considered. Maheu never saw Hughes face-to-face. He only communicated over the phone or by memo. I wondered, could some of the phone calls from Hughes to Maheu have originated from outside the Desert Inn?

Maheu couldn't testify in the trial that he spoke with Hughes on the phone during any evening in late December. It's important to remember how Hughes slipped out of the Desert Inn without Maheu's knowledge in 1970 when he left

Las Vegas. It's only reasonable to conclude that he could have slipped out before that time as well.

• • •

Chester Davis was Hughes's general counsel. He worked in close association with Bill Gay, chief of Hughes's operations, and Nadine Henley, who had evolved into an executive. They essentially took over Summa Corporation, Hughes's umbrella holding company. I've located information where Hughes was handed incorporation papers on December 21, 1972, and was asked to sign them. Hughes, seeing the new name of the corporation asked, "What the hell is Summa? How the hell do you pronounce it?" Clearly, he had lost control of his empire by this time.

Davis was a high-flying New York lawyer who was known for his damage control skills and his ruthless approach. He had actually only seen Hughes face-to-face four times during his many years of service. The Hughes corporations compensated him very well in legal fees. In the past, he had coordinated as many as fifty-six lawyers during the TWA hearings and negotiations. His budget for this assignment was twenty-five million dollars. He also controlled a group of operatives, frequently described as henchmen by those touched by them. Davis was the steel fist inside the velvet glove.

He would have had motivation for fighting against the Mormon Will. He was sitting pretty. He was general counsel for a major corporation. He had the inside track to those who ran the corporation, and he had become a multi-millionaire. He had no reason to believe that he would lose his position unless the will was found to be authentic.

Although he was included in the will as a key man in the company, he would have lost his substantial power within the organization. He had every motive to defeat the will at all cost.

It should be recalled that one of the envelopes given to Forsythe by Hughes was to be mailed to Chester Davis upon Hughes's death. This was done. We'll never know what the letter said, but we can draw some inferences. Hughes probably told Davis about the will and Melvin, and asked him to insure that his wishes be honored. Hughes never understood what kind of a man Davis was, and that he would do exactly the opposite.

Davis probably enlisted his operatives on his dark mission. It's possible that they were behind the destruction of the Hughes daily activity logs, the threat to Forsythe, tampering with the jury, and probably the perjured testimony of the aides as well. There is no indication that the contestants knew about these outrageous activities.

• • •

The Brigham Young University special collections library was quiet, and the light of the microfilm reader glowed in the dim of the room. The ghostly images of the reader were a bit fuzzy. Many of the documents had black streaks covering names and information found to be sensitive by the FBI employee who prepared the Howard Hughes file for dissemination, pursuant to a Freedom of Information Act request. I felt a little like a monk, cloistered in my cubicle copying by the dim light of a candle. The file contained investigation about Hughes, his TWA dealings, allegations of fraud, allegations of his kidnapping, submissions of various wills, and news articles. It also contains FBI laboratory requests and reports used in the probate trial. There was very little new information in the file, as it was originally opened as an administrative matter by the FBI and was essentially a repository of unrelated information regarding Howard Hughes.

One item of interest was reliance on information provided by LeVane Forsythe about the disappearance of Hughes from Las Vegas. He was clearly considered to be reliable by the FBI. The Bureau had chased Hughes to the Bahamas after Maheu's allegations of Hughes being kidnapped in 1970 surfaced, and they had determined that Hughes was alive and under his own control.

• • •

I spoke with a person who asked not to be identified, who had been associated with the Hughes Corporation. There was serious reluctance to provide information about Hughes. I promised, "I'll never reveal the source of your information. I'm looking for information that Hughes left the Desert Inn while he lived in Las Vegas. Do you know anything about it?"

"There were always rumors to that effect. Some of the stories were so ridiculous that we had a good laugh about them, but sometimes the rumors sounded reasonable."

"What about Edwin Daniel testifying that he saw Hughes at the Mizpah Hotel in Tonopah?" I asked.

The informant sighed. "That wouldn't surprise me a bit. Meier and his mining men spent a great deal of time there. They had permanent rooms in the hotel. It was their favorite haunt. They were big shots there.

"They threw a lot of money around. There was a great deal of talk at the Mizpah that Mr. Hughes would leave the Desert Inn and disappear for a time."

"All right, let's lay our cards on the table. Did you see Hughes outside the Desert Inn?"

After a long pause, the source responded, "No, but Larry Smith said he saw Hughes in Tonopah."

"That's interesting. Who is Larry Smith?"

"He was a mining consultant. He worked with John

Meier and helped find mining properties to buy. He said Mr. Hughes had been in Tonopah checking out mines he wanted to buy. He had seen him there."

"How do you know he said that?" I asked.

"Because he told me."

"Do you believe him?"

"Yes, I do."

I've searched for Larry Smith. He was a mining engineer and consultant who operated out of Salt Lake City in the 1960s. He was knowledgeable about mining. He didn't last long in an environment of greed and manipulation, so he left. My efforts to locate him have been unsuccessful. He is thought to be dead. Time has taken another valuable witness.

Melvin's sister-in-law received a telephone call that awakened her from a deep sleep sometime around 2001. The caller was a woman who sounded like she had been drinking. The caller slurred her words slightly as she explained, "I'm divorced from one of Hughes's bodyguards. You need to know that my ex told me that Hughes left the Desert Inn and got lost in the desert and Melvin Dummar picked him up."

Melvin's sister-in-law gave the woman Melvin's telephone number, but she never called him. I've tried to identify the night caller but, frustratingly, I've been unsuccessful.

The Mormon Will bequeathed a great deal of money to schools and organizations that could have done untold good for mankind, but the trial found that the estate should go to Lummis and other relatives who built a financial empire with the inheritance.

William Lummis had become a big game hunter. He had won the probate trial. Now he turned his sights on another elephant, the Summa Corporation. Gay and Davis thought they were safe. They had assumed that they would continue in their positions, but their strategic planning was thwarted when the jury ruled in favor of Lummis. A long and tempestuous trial resulted in Summa Corporation, along with seven casinos, and thousands of acres of land in the Las Vegas valley going to Lummis. Gay, Henley, and Davis were out. Eventually, the aides lost their lifetime consulting fees. Summa Corporation had imploded.

According to the Nevada State Revised Statutes, an inheritance claim must be filed within ninety days of the death of the grantor, in this case, Howard Hughes. This means that no new claims can be brought against the will by anyone. I wonder if obstruction of justice, perjury, jury tampering, witness intimidation, and subornation of perjury (soliciting someone to lie) during the trial would be grounds for ordering a new trial?

• • •

"The Hughes probate trial was a big one. There was a lot of interest in it for many years, and we kept the evidence in our vault for a long time. There hasn't been any activity for years, and since we have limited space in the evidence vault, eventually we destroyed it." These unfortunate words came from a deputy clerk of the Clark County Court.

I was stunned. "What was actually destroyed?" I asked.

"The transcripts, the original attorney filings, other documents, and all the evidence. We have kept copies of the original will in the file, but it shows stains from fingerprint chemicals," she replied, somewhat surprised by my question.

I asked, "Does that mean that the envelopes are gone?"

She looked at me questioningly. "Yes."

"It was my hope that we could do a DNA analysis on the envelopes. The saliva from sealing the envelopes would either be from Howard Hughes or someone else. This could have proven once and for all if Hughes had anything to do with the will!"

The clerk just stared at me, the implication sinking into her mind.

In early 2004, Melvin informed me that he had heard a rumor that the original Hughes's will was hanging on an attorney's office wall. My first thought was, how could this be possible if the Clark County Court deputy clerk destroyed it. Of course it could be possible for a deputy clerk to make a few bucks by putting the will aside and then reporting it destroyed. Later the will could be sold or auctioned to an interested party. This lead had to be followed up because, if the original will existed, then the original will envelope might also exist.

I left my home with high hopes. Unfortunately, the framed will hanging in the attorney's office was a copy and not the original. The attorney said, "I wish it was the original."

I assured him I did as well.

8

Howard's Road

M ost criminal investigations begin at the crime scene. In this case there was no crime scene, but there was a rescue site, at least according to Melvin. If he were telling the truth about picking up Howard Hughes on a desert road, then I wanted to see it for myself. I wanted to get a feel for the place and walk the ground. Maybe the road would give up its secrets.

I drove north out of Las Vegas on Highway 95. I left the land of make-believe where everything was available, and passed into a realm where only the essentials of life are at hand.

Time passes slowly in the desert. The miles race by, but the scenery seldom changes. I was alone with my thoughts as I passed the Indian Springs Correctional Facility, and memories of my visit to the prison several years ago came to mind. The FBI had done a buy-bust on a drug dealer who ran a Vegas strip club. He was mobbed up and had vowed to his superiors that he would never deal in drugs again, but he broke his promise and then a Bonanno crime family member ordered his murder as punishment for breaking the rules. The dealer went into hiding and surrounded himself with some friends. One of those friends made the mistake of putting on the drug dealer's jacket and driving his car to the grocery store to buy ice cream.

The friend never came back from the store. The police found his body the next morning. His hands had been cuffed behind his back, and he had been shot in the head several times. We assumed he had been confronted by men posing as police officers. He was dumped in the desert outside of Las Vegas like a heavy bag of cement.

I had visited the dealer at Indian Springs in an effort to convince him that he was a dead man unless he turned to the FBI for help. He ended up rolling over and testified for the government in several cases, and he was placed in the witness protection program. Investigations are often redirected like that. The original focus shifts as new facts or opportunities arise. Maybe the rescue site would provide new information.

• • •

Nature had a large expanse of extra land, which it wedged in between California and Utah. Much of this land is essentially waterless and unusable. The average rainfall of Nevada is the lowest in the U.S. The Paiute Indians, a primitive tribe of hunter-gatherers, wandered the hills and valleys of this desolate land. They camped near desert seeps where life-giving groundwater bubbled to the surface. Wildlife was also drawn to the springs, and the Spanish explorers marked their travels by the locations of the sparsely dispersed springs. For example, it was a four-day ride on horseback from Devil's Hole to Tonopah Springs. If the rider was unable to carry enough water for the four-day trip, he and his mount would die.

There are wooded mountains, many rising to the sky, that seem to have been dropped into place from another world. Many of the ten thousand- to thirteen thousand-foot mountains harbor dense pine forests and snow-capped peaks. The Spaniards called them Sierra Nevada. The snow melts and runs in rivulets that expand into streams and feed ponds and lakes in some places, but by far the 110,540 square miles of Nevada is barren and waterless. Even the states that border Nevada have a barren buffer area of high mountain desert bearing descriptive names such as Muddy Mountains, Confusion Range, Funeral Mountains, and Furnace Creek. There are sixteen large counties in the state, but outside of three counties, the state is rural and nearly unpopulated.

Lake Tahoe, a blue diamond in an emerald forest, is nestled on the border of Nevada and California. Its drainage fuels the water needs of the metropolitan area of Reno and Carson City located in the northwest corner of the state. Irrigation quenches the needs for farms in and around this area.

In the south, at the point of the wedge, Nevada is divided from Arizona by the meandering Colorado River. This mighty river, the largest west of the Missouri, cuts deep into the sandstone and is a ribbon of life in an otherwise parched, stone-hard land. The exploring Spaniards called this area Las Vegas, meaning "The Meadows." The Meadows was a patch of lush grass and cottonwood trees fed by a series of natural springs.

This became an oasis for Indians, explorers, Mormon settlers, and men looking to make their fortunes. The Mormons built an adobe fort to guard against Indian attacks, but they eventually found the land to be fruitless and abandoned their plans.

A few businesses sprang up—bars, brothels, and stores. These served the pioneers traveling the Spanish Trail to the gold fields and rich farm fields of California. The railroad came and brought goods from the East. Some of the weary travelers stopped in Las Vegas and settled there. Nevada received statehood on Halloween, 1864. It is the seventh largest state in the nation.

Historically, there have been two divergent cultures in Nevada. The North was punctuated by cattle wars and mining disputes. Fiercely independent men struggled to survive and to make themselves rich. Cattle and sheep roamed the sparse high plains and competed for the little forage available to them. The sheep ravaged the land because they pull up the brush and grass by its roots. This results in the denuding of the land. The cattle ranchers despised the sheep ranchers for this, and many sheep were shot and left to rot. The cattlemen also fought each other over grazing territory. There was little or no law out in the wide expanses of the high desert.

Even today, there are serious disputes over grazing rights. The federal government owns eighty-seven percent of the state. The Bureau of Land Management leases out huge parcels of land for grazing, but because of environmental concerns, roads have been blocked off and grazing rights have shrunk. This has resulted in a "sagebrush rebellion." The ranchers have taken the law into their own hands and reopened the roads and have grazed their cattle without permission. Two Indian sisters have recently had their cattle seized, but the battle goes on.

Nevada has always had its own mystique. Mark Twain, in his book *Roughing It*, wrote in 1872, Nevada is a place where "... the lawyer, the editor, the banker, the chief desperado, the chief gambler, and the saloon keeper occupied the same level of society, and it was the highest."

Paved roads branch off Tonopah Highway (Highway 95), which is the artery that feeds western Nevada. One leads east to the heavily guarded Atomic Energy Test Site where atomic bombs were tested in 1966 and 1967. Howard Hughes was very concerned with the fallout from the bombs while he lived in the Desert Inn and fought against the testing. Another road runs west across the California border to Death Valley. This national park is 3.3 million acres of parched, sun-bleached terrain. The annual rainfall is two inches. As you pass over the Funeral Mountains you drop from an altitude of five thousand four hundred feet above sea level to two hundred and eighty-two feet below sea level, the lowest point in the Western Hemisphere. The low humidity of Death Valley sucks the moisture out of life. The heat in summer often exceeds one hundred and twenty degrees, and the craggy overlook called Dante's View conjures up the scenes Dante saw in the infernos of hell.

In addition, there are literally dozens of dirt roads that come off the three hundred-mile stretch of highway between Gabbs and Las Vegas and run to the mountains on both sides of the road. Most of these roads lead to abandoned mines. The road where Melvin picked up the unconscious man is in Esmeralda County, Nevada, approximately one hundred and fifty-nine miles from Las Vegas. I've decided to call this "Howard's Road."

From my research of Hughes, it's clear that he flew over the boundless tracts of western Nevada in the summer of 1943. He would have been very familiar with the area, and if he had been in the desert in December of 1967, it would not have been a totally foreign place. He knew about the small, no-traffic-light towns scattered on the desert floor, isolated and widely dispersed. If Hughes had been in the desert, what was it that drew him? What would have had enough value for him to risk the trip?

I had made arrangements with Melvin to meet him in the parking lot of the Cottontail Ranch. After searching for a time, he located the remnants of Howard's Road. "I can't believe it's almost gone!" he exclaimed.

The road leads to the west, but rain and wind have smoothed the ruts, and the desert has reclaimed its own. I would never have noticed the remains of the road without Melvin's direction, though there are still some signs of the old trail, especially in the open areas of hard pack where nothing grows. I found an amber Hiram Walker & Sons Canadian Club Whiskey bottle lying where some traveler had discarded it years ago. When I checked with the company, I discovered that the whiskey company last used this particular type of bottle in the 1970s. If the wind and rain could erase some marks of man's passage, the desert could also preserve others. Perhaps if Howard Hughes had crashed his car in this area, it would still be here.

Melvin pointed to the western mountains and explained that the old road had run west. A 1965 Geological Survey map and a 1976 Defense Mapping Agency map are nearly identical with regard to Howard's Road. It's shown as an unimproved surface road leading to a gravel pit approximately three-quarters of a mile west of Highway 95.

That morning, summer monsoons had dropped fresh rain on this piece of the desert. The usual hard pack had been moistened and the air smelled clean. The temperature had dropped from one hundred and three to eighty-four degrees in a matter of minutes. These monsoons are born in the Pacific Ocean, and when the moist air travels over the heated desert, it comes as a gathering coalition of clouds. The ominous dark mass carries rain that may spill down in torrents or evaporate before it hits the ground. The black clouds are unpredictable and carry with them self-contained weather systems; anything from hail to microburst wind is possible. These winds often come like unexpected visitors. Everything is quiet, and suddenly ferocious gusts of sixty to seventy miles per hour winds come up and stir the desert dust into an impenetrable cloud. At times, lightning cracks like a jagged bullwhip in the darkened sky, but there is no rain. In the desert this is known as dry lightning, and these strikes often cause wildfires.

Howard's Road is approximately seven and a half miles south of the Cottontail Ranch. The valley is flat, making the canopy of trees surrounding the brothel visible to the north. "At night, the lights from the Cottontail are very bright," Melvin explained. "You can see it for miles." I thought of the lighthouses I had seen at night. In this case, the Cottontail Ranch was our lighthouse, a point of reference in the endless desert.

If Hughes wasn't dumped by someone, where was he going? What could have been so important to him? If he was headed for the mountains, what was he looking for? Melvin's story wouldn't make any sense unless I was able to find an answer to those questions. Melvin had left me to service his meat delivery route, so I drove north three miles until I found a passable road. Here, the dirt was hard and crusty; the monsoon had passed over without dropping its cargo of rain. The landscape was dotted with gray-colored sage and short brown scrub, nearly dead from lack of water. A gentle breeze eased the intense heat. The sky was a faded gray with menacing black clouds. Small, jagged rocks stuck out of the dirt like warts on the face of the desert. The only trees visible were in the small grove of cottonwoods sheltering the Cottontail Ranch.

I began to drive west on the hard-packed dirt road as it eased to the left. My SUV four-by-four handled the bumps well. After about a mile I came across an old ranch with a weathered gray cedar fence, dilapidated and fallen down in places. Some sections of the fence were completely gone, probably used for firewood over the years. A tall, gray, steel windmill tower made of sheet metal now bent and twisted stood like a sentinel behind the partial fence. In the past, the windmill had provided the power to run a pump supplying precious water to cattle, but this site had long been abandoned, and a golden eagle had taken advantage of the high tower and built its nest on the windmill platform. As I approached, the great raptor took flight from the platform and circled the area slowly, as if flying sentry duty. The entire basin around the ranch was flat and covered in dry range grass. It looked as though it had once been a lake bed. Alkali flats deposited along what must have been a lakeshore looked like patches of plaster. Climate and geological changes had removed the lake centuries ago.

I continued driving as the road eased to the southwest. The surface turned to washboard as it began to ascend slightly. A tiny desert chipmunk scurried across the road in front of me. Its little tail pulled into a white ball, and then as if struck by some schizophrenic urge, it ricocheted back across the road. I had to slow down to avoid crushing it under the tires.

Much of Nevada is a harsh, steel-hard land, but as you come closer you discover a unique ecosystem of interdependent life forms, perfectly equipped for desert survival. The desert is a marvel. There are insects in abundant variety and all manner of reptiles and small rodents. When the sun goes down, the predators come out to hunt: bats, snakes, coyotes, badgers, and owls, stalking in the night, searching for a meal. If you're lucky, you might see wild burros browsing in the sparse grass.

I had driven five miles when the landscape began to change. As the road got steeper, small gullies and washes appeared on both sides of the road. These funnel the run-off water as it cascades down the hard desert crust after heavy rains. The desert floor doesn't absorb much moisture, so the water often runs in torrents during storms. As I climbed higher, Joshua tree cacti with their outstretched arms welcomed me and became more and more abundant. The gullies and washes grew deeper, and at six miles, I came to a fork in the road. I decided to follow the fork to the right and found an abandoned mine, its white tailing piled up in a large mound. There was no sign of life so I returned to the fork and took a left hand swing deeper into the rolling mountains. I was now five thousand three hundred and eighty-eight feet above sea level. As I continued driving, it dawned on me that I had never been in mountains that didn't have at least some trees on them. I wondered if this is what the mountains of purgatory would look like. I began to believe that Hughes had never gotten this far into the mountains. He could never have driven this road in a luxury Chrysler, and since he was found just off Highway 95, it is doubtful that he had walked this far.

I came across stone cairns, indicating mining claims, along the road. A five-inch long lizard scurried down the face of one I stopped briefly to examine. These mini-towers of natural stone had been stacked carefully years ago by men who wanted it known that they owned the area. Each mound was a testament to countless hours of digging and hauling discarded stone. There were remnants of mine timbers, dried and partially buried. There were mounds of tailing all over the mountainside. This had clearly been a thriving mining area in years past, with as many as forty or fifty abandoned mines in this section of mountain alone.

At seven miles, the road became nearly impassable. My four-wheel drive Dodge churned on, but I could see it was becoming a road of no return. My map showed that it looped to the east around Mount Dunfee. I continued driving past other mining properties with brown, red, and yellow tailing mounds. All the mineshafts were filled in and the mines were abandoned. The road became more faint as the desert filled it in, and it swung west up the mountainside toward a town called Gold Point.

It had numerous steep dips and treacherous turns and hadn't been driven on for many years. Luckily, I was able to turn around, and I retraced my journey. As I returned to the six-mile point, the valley below was clear. I could see Highway 95, the beginning of the ranch road, and parts of Howard's Road as well as the trees of the Cottontail Ranch.

I was convinced that if Hughes had driven Howard's Road in December of 1967, he would have needed a truck or a jeep. But there is no evidence that he ever had a jeep or a truck, so I had to assume he drove his Chrysler. If he had been injured while in the mining area in the dark, he would have seen the lights of the Cottontail Ranch, and the headlights of the passing cars on Highway 95 would have drawn him. However he came to the area, he must have come in a vehicle of some kind, and if he left in Melvin's Chevy

Caprice, his vehicle would have stayed in the desert. But there was no sign of a wrecked car or of rusted auto parts along the road or in any of the gullies. Had it been towed away years ago? Or did one of Hughes's employees pick up the car and drive it back to Las Vegas?

I looked out over the valley, but there was nothing to see for miles. The hot breeze flowed over me like heat from a sauna, but my mind was in overdrive. If Melvin had made up the story about picking up Hughes, why would he pick this godforsaken spot? It would be more logical to say he picked up the old man somewhere near a town. At least there would be some sense to that. This place didn't make sense.

Everyone had doubted Melvin's story because it was so improbable, but that's the reason I believe him. If you were to make up a story to explain how you met Howard Hughes, wouldn't you make something up that people could easily believe? Any sane person would, and Melvin is certainly sane. But why was Hughes here?

Seeing the Cottontail Ranch from the mountaintop reminded me that I needed to make inquiries there. Under the heading "Brothels," the 2002 Nevada West Yellow Pages had the following ad: "The Cottontail Ranch, Madam Beverly Harrell's world-famous legal bordello, open 24 hours, bar, gift shop, 2 mile airstrip. Same owner, same location for 33 years." If Madame Harrell has been in business that long, maybe she would know something about Hughes visiting her establishment.

I tried to imagine if the Cottontail could be involved. A dirt airstrip runs diagonally away from the Cottontail. Could Hughes have flown in from Las Vegas and crashed in attempting to land on the two-mile runway, causing his head injury? It would not have been the first time that Hughes had done so. Or maybe, instead of him crashing a vehicle in the mountains, Hughes had been to the Cottontail and had an altercation with someone. Maybe he had staggered through the desert, seven and a half miles south, and collapsed. Perhaps he was dumped by someone from the Cottontail and was left to die. These scenarios are improbable, as we know that at that point in his life Hughes was reclusive and secretive in every way. He was also an avowed teetotaler at that point and hated social interaction. Even though it was an improbable scenario, it had to be checked out. Investigative tunnel vision had already stifled the truth, and I wanted to consider every possibility, no matter how unlikely.

The Cottontail is a white frame building with a gravel drive and large parking lot. The lot is big enough to hold a convention. There were two cars parked in front, which, I assumed, belonged to customers. I climbed four wooden stairs to the front door. It opened easily into a small waiting area. There was a locked door with a small glass window directly in front of me and a doorbell to the right of the door with a hand-lettered sign indicating the brothel was closed and "the girls are on vacation." I wondered what the girls did on their vacations.

I rang the bell, and a woman came to the door. She was much too young to be the famous proprietor. When I asked for Madame Harrell, the woman stated that she had died "six years ago" and that the house was now under new ownership and was closed temporarily. I said, "Your ad says Madame Harrell is the proprietor."

The woman gave me a scornful look and shrugged. So much for truth in advertising. I asked if she had ever heard rumors of Howard Hughes being at the brothel many years ago. She responded dully, "Who's Howard Hughes?" Apparently, they don't make madams the way they used to.

Obviously, the two cars in the lot belonged to the proprietor and not to customers.

• • •

Some weeks later, I learned that a man named Hank Dahlstrom had operated Dahlstrom's Garage in the late 1960s out of Goldfield, Nevada. He would have towed most wrecked cars in the area. In an effort to locate Dahlstrom, I drove to Goldfield.

Highway 375 is a surgical incision across the midsection of Nevada. The highway has been officially designated the "Extraterrestrial Highway" by the state. The locals (tongue-in-cheek) have long claimed that aliens and spacecraft are kept at a secret facility, known as Area 51, on the Atomic Energy Test Site south of the highway. The Nevada Test Site, larger than the state of Rhode Island, is a massive outdoor laboratory and experimental center. The test site, Nellis Air Force Base bombing range, and the nuclear repository facility known as Yucca Mountain are all located in the region. A Nevada Senator once referred to Yucca Mountain, in disgust, as "the nuclear suppository."

If aliens did visit this bleak land, they would surely be disappointed. Every section of the country has its folklore, and the few people who inhabit the area have created this folklore for commercial purposes. They sell Area 51 T-shirts, alien coffee mugs, and other trinkets to supplement their income.

I didn't see any aliens, but I did see a dead cow along the road outside of Goldfield. It was bloated like a helium balloon. Coal black ravens perched patiently on fence posts like morticians as turkey buzzards sailed the wind currents, circling the carcass. When the heat had finished its work, they would feast.

Esmeralda County is about halfway down the angled

western side of Nevada. The county's western edge, the state line, includes Nevada's highest peak. There are five towns in the entire county, with Goldfield being the largest. There are no roadside rest stops, no lavatories, no shaded areas to find relief. Like the land, there is nothing hospitable about this region of Nevada.

I arrived in Goldfield in the afternoon. The sun was beating down like a hammer as I drove down the main road of the little town. Main Street is part of Highway 95 and cuts Goldfield in two. There isn't a single traffic light in town, and most of the public buildings are boarded up. There are houses and mobile homes on patches of desert on both sides of the highway. Few have cultivated yards. Most of the side roads are paved with gravel.

I was shopping for information. As I pulled into town, I saw a man sitting in a lawn chair across from one of the boarded up buildings. He was seated in front of a small convenience store. He waved to cars as they passed, and appeared to be a man who knew what was going on in the small community. The man had a long gray beard and a protruding belly that gave the impression that he was hiding two watermelons under his XXXL white T-shirt.

"How you doing?" I asked as I approached him. He nodded in response.

"I'm looking for Hank Dahlstrom. You know where I can find him?" I queried.

"Yup, he just passed as you crossed the street."

I looked down the road and saw an old green truck turn left off Main Street onto a side road. "Is that him?" I asked as I pointed to the turning truck.

"Yup, he picks up his wife every day, and then they go back to his place."

"Where's his place?" I asked.

"He lives in his old garage. He used to operate a gas station and garage years ago, and now he lives there. It's right down the road." He pointed north on Main Street.

"He and his wife live separately?" I asked incredulously.

The man folded his arms across his substantial belly and smiled.

"Yup. Kind of strange, ain't it? He sees her every day about this time. Like I said, he picks her up, and they go back to his place for awhile. Then he takes her home."

I asked, as an afterthought, "You ever hear of Howard Hughes being in the Goldfield area years ago?"

He looked at me in a strange way, as if he couldn't compute the connection between Dahlstrom and Hughes. "No, never heard of that," he responded.

"Thanks for your help," I said to the unofficial tourist greeter. He was accustomed to providing information and not asking any questions. I had gotten the information I needed, and returned to my car.

I found the faded green Willy's shortbed jeep pickup parked in front of an old mobile home deposited in a patch of brown dead weeds. I could feel the burning heat of the midday sun as I got out and made my way around a large plastic garbage bag stuffed with empty beer cans. I knocked on the door and a moment later, was welcomed in by an elderly lady. A man I took to be Dahlstrom was seated on a couch with a TV tray in front of him, munching on chocolate chip cookies and drinking beer. I introduced myself and told him I was looking into past mining operations in the area. I asked if he was Hank Dalhstrom.

He said he was. I inquired if he would mind answering a few questions about his old towing business. He shook his head. He didn't seem concerned as to why I wanted to question him about it. I guess he was happy just to have something to talk about. The sun was baking outside, but I wasn't offered a drink.

"I understand that you ran a tow company in the late sixties. Is that right?"

He took a bite of a cookie and answered, "Oh, I started long before that."

"Were you the only guy towing cars back then?"

"Pretty much," he responded.

I nodded. "Do you remember towing a vehicle out of the dirt road about seven miles south of the Cottontail Ranch in late 1967 or early 1968?"

He sat and thought for awhile. He took another bite. "I towed a lot of cars out of that area. That's out by Gold Point, ain't it?"

Dahlstrom looked to be about seventy-five years of age. He was fairly tall, maybe five foot ten. He looked to be in good shape for his age. I answered, "Yes it is, but I'm talking about east of Gold Point. There was a dirt road that ran up into the mountains. There are mines at the end of the road there."

"I towed a lot of cars over the years. All them dirt roads lead to mines. That's why they made the roads. Took some from the Gold Point area." He took another bite. His fingers were dirty with engine grease.

"Do you remember a vehicle in a ditch or on the dirt road this side of Gold Point?" I asked, trying to be as patient as possible.

"I'm not sure."

I continued. "Do you remember towing a vehicle for Howard Hughes from that area?"

Dahlstrom wasn't a man who showed any emotion. "I

don't remember that," he responded. I thought, at least someone knows who Howard Hughes was around here.

"Would you have records from that time period?"

"No, records are only a problem. The tax people always check your records."

I thought I'd give it one more try. "Do you remember hearing anything about Howard Hughes being in this area or wrecking a car around here?"

He took a long swig from his beer bottle, then set it down. He wiped his hands on his blue, grease-stained coveralls. "Nope."

I had hit a dead end. Of course dead ends are really only detours. If you're going to pursue an investigation, a dead end just pushes you in a new direction. It eliminates certain possibilities. I had learned a few things from my visit to the desert. One was that I believed Melvin, if only because no one would make up a story about finding Howard Hughes in that wasteland. Another thing was that the only thing of any potential value in the area that could attract someone like Hughes was a mine. Mines were everywhere, most of them now played out, to be sure. But what were they like in 1967? Could it be possible that Hughes left his Desert Inn Hotel suite to look at mines in the Nevada Desert?

Edwin Daniel, Hughes's director of engineering, had said to Dummar's lawyer that Hughes had disappeared from the Mizpah Hotel in Tonopah. Although he'd softened his story the next day in court, wincing from the bruises and cuts on his face, he had said there were mining people with Hughes at the Mizpah, so mines were involved somehow. I decided that Tonopah would be my next stop. It's the county seat for Nye County, approximately thirty-four miles north of Howard's Road on Highway 95.

Tonopah is nestled in a fold of treeless mountains. The tailing of long-abandoned mines, like large sand piles, forever scar the hillsides. I drove down Main Street past motels, stores, casinos, and the Mizpah Hotel, once the crown jewel of the region. It's closed and boarded up now, a testament to what had been. The hotel had five floors with forty-one rooms. The ground floor housed the hotel registration, a restaurant, bar, and casino. It was built in 1907 of native stone to accommodate wealthy miners and prominent travelers. It also accommodated Melvin Dummar on the night of December 29, 1967.

Legend has it that Tonopah Springs was a stopover for Indians, Spanish explorers, and pioneers. It was a welcome rest stop. The springs watered portions of the desert, creating patches of lush swamp grass and cattails that look like gardens in a moonscape. Then in 1902, a man named Jim Butler was looking for a lost mule in the area and came upon a rock formation containing gold. The rush was on. A large town sprang up, eventually taking the Indian name for the area, and even Wyatt Earp, the famous gun fighter and lawman, resided there for a time. After the gold rush ended, the town stagnated. Now, it's a stopover between Las Vegas and Reno. The town recalls its headier days in the Tonopah Historic Mining Park, located on the site of the Mizpah Mine. The road leading to the mine is Summa Hill Road, named after the Summa Corporation, the holding company for Hughes's business empire.

Bob Perchetti, a local entrepreneur and owner of the Club House Bar in Tonopah, has been around a long time and is familiar with the history and the characters of the area. He has a fascination with Howard Hughes and wants to revitalize Tonopah and hopes to establish a Howard Hughes museum and wedding chapel. He's recognized as the local expert on Howard Hughes. It seemed logical to debrief him. He told me that the people who owned the Mizpah Hotel in 1967-68 were now dead, and he couldn't think of anyone who was employed there during that time period.

He said the Hughes Corporation established an office to handle its mining business in a building behind his club in the late sixties. He recalled rumors that Hughes had returned to Tonopah to visit mines his company had purchased, but Perchetti could never pin down the source of the rumors. When I asked him if he thought it was possible that Hughes could have personally visited mines, he responded, "It's possible, but he was so secretive that he probably would have done it at night in the dark."

I was enjoying my time with Bob Perchetti, and I let him talk. I've learned that you never know where your next lead will come from, and at last I had found someone who knew a great deal about Howard Hughes and even a bit about Melvin Dummar. For instance, he remembered that Melvin had been invited to perform at the Mizpah Hotel, in celebration of Jim Butler Days in the late 1970s because of his notoriety during the Hughes probate trial. Melvin has always been a wanna-be country western singer, and he savored this opportunity. Perchetti also explained that, contrary to many of the Hughes's biographies, Hughes hadn't married Jean Peters, his second wife, in the Mizpah Hotel, but rather at the L and L Motel, in room number thirty-three. The L and L offered the only other lodging in Tonopah at the time. The wedding was a typical Hughes performance. The only people allowed at the wedding were two Hughes aides and the justice of the peace who performed the ceremony. Hughes and Peters both used assumed names, and to complete the masquerade, even the justice of the peace used an alias when signing the marriage license.

The owner of the motel at the time was a man named Leroy David (now deceased). I located a transcript of an oral history taken of David in 1988 as part of a project carried out by the Nye County Historical Society. Referring to the Mizpah Mine, he said, "I owned the mine about five or six years till I sold it through Clarence Hall to Howard Hughes. He has had it ever since then. Of course I had a lot of property for real estate. The only thing I have done that was good on real estate was own the mine and selling it."

I also obtained a map of the locations of mines from the historical society. Black dots, designating mines, covered the map. It looked like someone had sprayed the paper with ink. If Hughes had purchased mines in Nye County there should be a record of the acquisitions in the county recorder's office, so that was my next stop. The handwritten entries in the recorder's books filled page after page. Beginning on July 23, 1969, the Hughes Tool Company had purchased over one hundred mines. But none prior to that time. Nonetheless, the date was so tantalizingly close to the date Melvin says he picked Hughes out of the desert that I couldn't stop there. If this was a dead end, I was going to make sure it was absolutely dead.

• • •

The man who would know about Hughes's Nevada holdings in 1967 and 1968 is Robert Maheu. He had acquired seven casinos for his boss and vast tracts of raw land around Las Vegas. If Hughes was personally involved in the purchase of mines, Maheu should know about it. Maheu, who still lives in Las Vegas, told me that in 1967, the United States needed gold and silver. Its reserves were running low, and the price of both had soared. I was aware that the mountains of Nevada—the Silver State—contained ample supplies of each. I was also aware from my earlier historical research that Hughes's father had often described the mines of western Nevada to his son. He told him stories of adventure and exploration in the area. He once wrote "… I would like to seek my fortune under the surface of the earth." He even did some mining in Colorado and Oklahoma. Hughes's interest in Nevada mines was understandable.

Maheu told me that he had discussed the mines of Nevada with Hughes. A memorandum sent to Hughes by Maheu on March 16, 1968, reads "Because of the gold situation and since we know where the proven gold deposits and reserves are in the state of Nevada, what do you think of the possibility of our moving expeditiously and tying them up forthwith?" In another memo, he also informed Hughes that one of their employees, John Meier, "had, in fact, obtained some options on, I believe, one specific property which included a lot of claims…"

Hughes responded quickly in a handwritten memo. "This sounds good, why don't you find out specifically what we can tie up and upon what terms. However, why don't you let me know first from your own knowledge—before you make inquiries. I would hate to attract somebody else to these gold properties before we are ready to move in any substantial degree."

Maheu confirmed what the memos said. "We bought a couple or three properties we thought were good acquisitions." But he couldn't recall how he learned about the mines, whom he'd dealt with, or where they were located. He said that he believed that John Meier was somehow involved in these early purchases.

Meier was a thirty-four-year-old Long Island native and a former life insurance manager. He had been brought to Las Vegas at the urging of Bill Gay, for whom he'd worked at a firm called Hughes Dynamics in California. Gay was the chief executive officer for Hughes's various businesses and had gotten ahead of himself in setting up a new company without the approval of the boss. Hughes had learned of the unauthorized company, and in a fit of anger, had demanded that it be closed. Gay told Maheu that Meier had two doctorate degrees and his wife had cancer, so he needed a job. Hughes apparently knew about Meier because he encouraged Maheu to hire him. Realistically, Maheu had no choice. At Hughes'ss request, and because of Meier's education, Meier was assigned to fight atomic testing in Nevada. Hughes was paranoid about nuclear fallout and was convinced that atomic detonations at the test site would damage Las Vegas. Maheu said he "put him on the payroll as my scientific advisor." Then on or about April 17, 1968, Hughes placed John Herbert Meier in charge of mining acquisition and operations. He acquired mines and potential mines for Hughes all over Nevada. The claims were scattered in Clark, Churchill, Mineral, Esmeralda, Lyon, Humboldt, and Nye counties. In all, he purchased over two hundred properties for the price of about twenty million dollars.

On December 30, 1967, one day after Melvin reported picking up the old man, Hughes wrote the following memo. "Make sure please we have the Houston firm's promise of secrecy. From everyone! Tell him again at the end, and tell him I have additional property to acquire in that area and any leakage of these plans - boom - impossible." Could this memo refer to the mine acquisitions Hughes wanted to keep secret?

At the time, an old-timer knowledgeable about mining in Nevada speculated in a newspaper interview that Hughes must have developed some new system of extracting ore in a more economical way because "most of the mines have collapsed. The equipment isn't any good; it's old, rusted, and worthless. I can't imagine what the man is up to. Maybe he plans to go into mining, maybe he doesn't."

In a January 9, 1969 memo to Hughes I found among trial documents, Meier wrote that the Hughes Nevada operations, "... have now acquired approximately one half the area of Tonopah Mining, some in Nye County, and some in Esmeralda. This consists of approximately eighty percent of known silver reserves in the area." The mines were not limited to gold and silver, but almost anything that could be considered a mining claim was picked up, including copper claims.

Now I felt I was very close to the date Melvin said he found Hughes. If Meier had acquired "one half" of Tonopah Mining by January of 1969, where were these mines? I knew they weren't in Nye County. I had seen the records. They must have been in Esmeralda County, and maybe Hughes went to see them.

These early mine acquisitions were secured by options to buy. Someone, probably Meier, entered into a thirty-day option agreement that held the property until it could be scouted and examined. Of course, another reason for not divulging the identity of the true buyer was that the asking price would be inflated at the mention of Hughes's name. If the property was acceptable, the option was executed, and the sale was finalized.

Several names come up time and again in my review of the mine deed records. They are Leonard Traynor, Clarence

Hall, Dennis Hill, and Eldon Cleveland (all deceased). Cleveland, a flashy guy who always carried five to ten thousand dollars in his pocket, started a business called Basic Industries in Tonopah and was a mining consultant to Meier. Hill and Hall (a geologist) were businessmen who acquired mines. Traynor was a deputy state mining inspector who knew Hill. These four characters could easily have been the "mining people" Edwin Daniel referred to seeing in the Mizpah Hotel in Tonopah. Unknown to Hughes at the time, Meier was also employed by Basic Industries and even owned stock in that company. So he was receiving a substantial salary from Hughes (the buyer) as well as from Basic Industries (the seller). They often purchased mining claims on one day and then turned around and sold them to Hughes at inflated prices at a later time.

For instance, Hughes Tool Company bought mining properties in Lyon and Storey counties, south of Virginia City, near American Flat. Known as the Comstock Lode, these properties were part of the most important and productive mining camp in the world from 1860 to 1880. The deeds to these properties are dated March 27, 1968. Cleveland obtained some of these mines for five hundred dollars by way of a quitclaim deed on March 25, 1968. The mines were sold to Hughes for two hundred and twenty-five thousand dollars.

Two weeks after the Comstock acquisitions, a memo addressed from Maheu was delivered to Hughes. It stated, "We obtained an option from Mr. and Mrs. Denny Hill last month on 240 acres of mining property including seven patented mines for $240,000 - estimated value of this property is 2 million. It is primarily composed of zinc, lead, and silver at Goodsprings in Clark County." This may have been one of the memos submitted to Hughes by Meier using Maheu's name. Hughes obviously knew who Dennis Hill was, since the memo mentions the name without any explanation and uses the personal "Denny," rather than "Dennis." Also, the memo shows Hughes being interested in the actual status and locations of the mines. He was clearly involved in the early "couple or three properties we thought were good acquisitions." Could it be that Hughes decided to explore a site or two for himself? Maybe he wanted to relive those great memories of his father's dreams that had excited him as a youth.

I now knew that Hughes Tool Company had purchased mines as early as March of 1968. John Meier seemed to be the link between Hughes and the mines. And Meier was one of the men Edwin Daniel named as having been at the Mizpah Hotel with Hughes the night he disappeared.

Maheu said, "Meier was too aggressive. He was hobnobbing with politicians, all kinds of people, including Don Nixon, the President's brother." He had no mining experience, and according to Maheu, he had no doctorate degrees either. During this period, Meier submitted memos to Hughes using Maheu's forged initials, thereby bypassing Maheu's review and scrutiny. Maheu learned that he was, "… practicing double escrows and essentially stealing from Hughes" and recommended several times that he be fired "for continuing indiscretions," but Hughes liked Meier, and for some unknown reason delayed authorizing his dismissal until November 15, 1969. Finally, when confronted by Maheu, Meier resigned. Later, a mining consultant and geologist submitted a report to Hughes Tool Company stating that of the one hundred and twelve mines he studied, "105 had no value in terms of recognizable mineral deposits." Eventually, Meier realized he was under investigation for embezzlement and tax violations and fled to Vancouver in 1972, knowing Canada wouldn't extradite tax evaders to the U.S. He and Eldon Cleveland were both indicted for tax evasion in 1973. Cleveland, who also fled to Canada, died that year.

Melvin's former attorney told me in 2003 that Meier had been interviewed in Vancouver, British Columbia prior to the probate trial. He told the lawyer he had proof that Hughes had left the Desert Inn, but he wanted to make a deal with the government before providing the information. He said he was willing to testify if the tax charges were dropped. No deal was struck. As a result, he refused to provide information that, he said, "… would prove Hughes left the Desert Inn and was picked up in the desert."

I made every effort to find Meier, but months passed and I heard nothing. I returned to finding the other links in the chain. Clearly, Hughes was acquiring mines all over Nevada in 1968, and the memos suggest that the search had begun earlier. But I had no evidence that Hughes had acquired mines in the area of Howard's Road at that time. It was back to Esmeralda County for me.

• • •

It's hard to imagine how bustling and hopeful Esmeralda County was during the height of the mining boom, or how quickly it faded. As I searched for anyone who could tell me about Hughes's mining acquisitions in the area, I made my way to Gold Point, high up on the mountain. Silver was discovered there in 1902, and tons of the mineral were mined until 1908. At its peak, Gold Point had two hundred and twenty-five wooden buildings, shacks, and tents housing miners and merchants. The Great Western Mine was the cornerstone of the community until 1942, when major mining efforts came to an end. Today Gold Point is a ghost town. Someone has made a valiant effort to restore it, but on the day I visited, there were no tourists. Only six people live there now.

One of those residents is Amarillo John. He's an old-timer in every sense of the word. He lives in one of the original wooden houses with gray tint that is evidence of its age. The house is no more than twenty feet by thirty feet in size and has a front porch screened in by chicken wire. I'd hate to see the flies in Gold Point if the large wire mesh is intended to keep them out. John is a very likable sort of guy, down to earth, living on bare necessities. I introduced myself and told him I was looking for someone who would know about mining in the area, especially in the late 1960s. He responded from inside the porch. "You're looking at him. I'm the only one left up here that knows about those days."

"There's no mining now, is there?" I asked.

"No, not any more. That's gone. Everything is gone, my wife is dead, and so are my friends. I tinker around and wait."

"What are you waiting for? You think the mining will come back?" I asked naively.

"Not unless there's some kind of miracle. It costs too much to pull the ore out and refine it. You can't make no money at it no more. No, I'm waiting to go to my wife. I came into this life with nothin', and I'm taking it all with me when I go." He grinned, exposing some missing teeth.

I smiled in return. "Have you ever heard of Howard Hughes owning any property up here somewhere?"

He nodded. "Sure, he had guys all over the place buying up mines in the late sixties. They even had an office over there." He pointed to the west. "It ain't there no more."

This piqued my interest. "Did you ever hear of him coming out here and inspecting any of the properties?" I asked hopefully.

"Nope, never heard about that, but who knows." Then, after giving some brief thought, he added, "I've got some claims on the other side of Mount Dunfee there." He pointed past Gold Point to the east.

Mount Dunfee rang a bell in my mind. It was a landmark I had noted on the map while driving the ranch road to the mountains. "Did Hughes own any mines down there?" I asked.

"Not that I know of, but there's a lot of mines down there. I don't know them all. Lemme show you something." He hurriedly returned to his house.

I wasn't sure if he was coming back or not, but I stood beside my Dodge and waited. A constant breeze was blowing, mercifully tempering the heat. As I looked toward the other wooden structures, I saw a covey of quail scurry across the gravel street. They were going somewhere in a hurry, but my investigation sure wasn't.

John returned, this time wearing a straw hat held together with duct tape. He must have thought the occasion warranted formal headwear. He was holding a large rolled paper. "This is a map of the area we were discussin'," he said as he unrolled the plot map. He laid it out on the hood of my vehicle, and we studied it like men planning a military campaign. Pointing to the map, John said, "These mines are all part of the old Goldcrest Mining Company. They're mine!" He beamed proudly.

"Did you ever mine them?" I asked.

"No, but maybe someday, if the price of gold jumps."

I thanked him and went on my way. I felt like I had wasted my time. But I took comfort in knowing that wasting your time came with the territory because every once in awhile, it wasn't a waste at all. You only find answers by looking and asking questions.

I drove to Goldfield to check the property records, that kind of tedious and mandatory research that is part of the investigator's daily bread and butter. Goldfield, Nevada is a bend in the road. It's a withering oasis in sagebrush-covered hills. A huge field of underground rock containing veins of gold was discovered nearby in 1902, giving the town its name. From 1903 to 1910, Goldfield was the largest city in Nevada, having an estimated population of twenty thousand people. Today, the current population of all of Esmeralda County is one thousand three hundred and forty people. Goldfield's mines produced more than eighty-six million dollars in gold and silver from 1903 to 1940. A series of fires and a flash flood destroyed much of the town in 1923. After World War II the price of silver dropped, which made mining unprofitable, and the city began to disappear. Today it's a living ghost town, hanging on by its fingertips, fighting to stave off disaster and despair. First the mines closed, then the motel, then the restaurant, then the businesses along Main Street, then the gas stations, and finally the grocery store. Even the tourist rock shops are closed.

Recently, an election for Esmeralda County commissioner ended in a dead heat. Each candidate received one hundred and seven votes. The deadlock was settled, Old West style, by a face-to-face draw of cards—high card wins.

Each candidate drew a jack, but based on the rules of the game, a spade beats a diamond. Democracy triumphed. The fact that the town survives at all is a testament to the resilience of the people living there. As Tonopah has become a stopover place, Goldfield is a passthrough place.

But Goldfield is the county seat of Esmeralda County, and it's where the property records are kept. The Goldfield Court House was built in 1907 of hand-hewn, native stone and contains county offices as well as the courthouse and jail. The interior is Victorian with hand carved wood paneling and Tiffany lamps. The first floor walls are covered with cattle brands burned into brown leather patches, a reminder of the open range days where every cattle rancher had to distinguish his cows from all the others grazing the range. The dark second floor hallway walls are covered with framed documents and historic black and white photographs.

The recorder's office is just as I would have pictured it. It's a large room divided into a central record room, a reception area, and a back vault. Shelves filled with large bound books are everywhere. There are several long wooden tables and waist-high pedestals for reading the large volumes. The actual office where the recorder sits is set up like an old bank, with a counter and a barred window opening. I doubt that it's been changed since 1907. The staff was very helpful and provided a great deal of assistance as I poured through the massive volumes.

The books that record land transactions are divided by year and are listed alphabetically by buyer. I went to the volume labeled 1966 through 1970. Twelve inches high by eighteen inches wide and four inches thick, it probably weighed eight pounds. It was black, trimmed in red, and the entries were handwritten in beautiful script. I carried it to the reading pedestal and set it down.

Under "H" I found no listing for Howard Hughes in

1966. I turned the page to 1967. Nothing. I turned to 1968, and in the middle of the page were the words "Hughes Tool Company." The company had obtained a deed for nine mines from the Arivaca Mining Company on October 15, 1968. This date, almost a year after Hughes was rescued on Howard's Road, didn't provide insight as to why he might be visiting Esmeralda County during the pertinent time period.

I kept going. Early the next year, on January 30, 1969, two property transfers were recorded. One purchase was from Dennis C. Hall and consisted of three mines. The other was purchased from Leonard Traynor, for two separate parcels consisting of many mines. Hughes's agent on the deeds was listed as Joseph Foley, a Las Vegas attorney, part of a family of attorneys. I called him, hoping he would be of some assistance. He could easily claim attorney-client privilege, but since his client, Howard Hughes, was dead, he might feel free to speak. I introduced myself and told him, "I'm doing some research on mines in Esmeralda County. I note that you're listed as agent for Hughes Tool Company on several mining transactions. Could I ask you who your client was back then?"

"It's none of your business!" he sputtered.

So much for the attorney-client argument. "Did you deal with Mr. Hughes himself or someone else?" I asked.

"It's none of your business!"

I asked, "I'd like to know how these transactions worked. Had the mines been inspected by someone before Hughes Tool Company bought them?"

He became more agitated. "Look, I don't have time for mysteries." The phone went dead.

Foley had testified against John Meier in the civil embezzlement trial, so he had already told his story in a public forum. Bob Maheu had also told me that he had dealt with Foley on the "couple or three properties" that he had discussed with Hughes.

I continued my archive search and went to another book where I looked up the actual deeds to the properties. Even though the Hall and Traynor sales were recorded on the same date, the actual deeds were not dated the same. The Hall deed was dated January 9, 1969. Not close enough to December 29, 1967 to be of value.

The date on the other deed jumped off the page. "This indenture, made and entered into this 24th day of January, 1968..." I whispered to myself, "Bingo!" The Hughes Tool Company had bought mines twenty-six days after Melvin says he picked up Hughes on Howard's Road. With the thirty-day option to buy, it would make the option valid from about December twenty-fourth through January twenty-fourth. The option would have made Hughes the owner of the mines on December 29, 1967.

I tried to imagine the events as they might have occurred. Hughes would, in all likelihood, have taken the first opportunity to see the mines for himself during the option period. He could potentially have visited these mines soon after Christmas of 1967.

I continued to read the deed. On the second page was a listing of the mines purchased: "... Sunrise No. 1 through 24... Starlite No. 1 through 6... Rex ... Great Western ... Ruby 1 and Ruby 2..." The Great Western mine was located on Gold Point, over the mountain from the ranch road. But there was another name I knew, and I suddenly blessed Amarillo John. One of the mines named on his map was the Sunrise. I'd noticed it when he showed me his map. The mine was located at the end of Howard's Road.

Why was the deed filed with the recorder's office a year later? Could it be that someone was trying to hide the fact that Hughes had bought mines in January of 1968? By filing the two deeds together, the one that was much earlier slipped through the system without notice.

Still, there were thirty-four mines listed in the Traynor deed. If the other thirty-three were somewhere else, I would be on shaky ground. Where were the Rex, Ruby, Starlite, and the other mines located? I walked down the hall to the assessor's office, where the plot maps showing locations of properties in Esmeralda County are kept. I looked up the coordinates of the various plots and located them on a large map of Esmeralda County hanging on the wall. The first mine, the Rex, was located west of Goldfield, nowhere near Howard's Road. I traced the coordinates for the Ruby mines. Both are at the end of Howard's Road. The same held true for the Starlite mines. Of the thirty-four mines purchased by Hughes Tool Company on January twenty-fourth, thirty-two were at the end of Howard's Road, and one was on Gold Point on the other side of the mountain. I had found a hidden piece of the puzzle. Now, I knew what could have drawn Hughes to western Nevada.

9

Three Witnesses

E very investigation leaves a sliver in your foot, an unanswered question that putrefies because of its importance to the case. The festering sliver in this case is John Meier, Hughes's chief of mining operations. He was running all over Nevada scouting mines and acquiring properties in 1967, 1968, and 1969. It's logical to infer that he can resolve many of the unanswered questions in this story. He most certainly holds several missing pieces of this investigative mosaic.

Did Howard Hughes leave the Desert Inn and go into the desert? Kay Glenn told me emphatically, "I'm telling you, Howard Hughes never left the confines of his suite at the Desert Inn Hotel while he lived in Las Vegas! Since he didn't leave, he couldn't have been in the desert, and since he wasn't in the desert, Melvin Dummar couldn't have picked him up."

Was Glenn's pronouncement true? If it was, why did he

tell Dr. Ford, "… Hughes would take off in the desert." John Meier could resolve this dilemma. He would know if Hughes had left his hotel room on the Strip.

My several efforts to locate and question John Meier were met with frustration until I received a message on my answering machine nearly ten months after the inception of my inquiry. The recorded message was, "I don't know if I have the right telephone number. My name is John Meier."

He left his phone number, and I called him as soon as I was able. We spoke, and after some small talk, I told him I was a retired FBI agent doing research into the Howard Hughes—Melvin Dummar affair. He said, "I have the highest respect for the FBI, as agents treated me with respect when they contacted me in the past."

I said, "I've been trying to get in touch with you for a long time. I know you were with Howard Hughes at the Mizpah Hotel in Tonopah, Nevada in late 1967 or early 1968."

His answer was remarkable in its simplicity. He acknowledged, "Yes, and it got Edwin Daniel beat up."

"Daniel said Hughes was with you at the Mizpah. Do you know who beat him up?" I asked.

"No, but there were many who didn't want him to testify."

I speculated, "That's what I thought. His testimony could have been devastating to the opponents of the will. He watered down his original statement because of the beating."

Meier didn't say anything. He was reluctant to speak over the telephone as he didn't know me, but I needed to know exactly what he could say about Hughes, so I asked him straight up. "What can you say about Hughes being out of the Desert Inn?"

He answered without hesitation. "Howard Hughes was

with me and others in the Tonopah area. We were looking at mines. He went out on his own and got lost." Meier hesitated for a second then added, "I've always felt sorry for Dummar because he got a bad deal."

There it was! After these many years, John Meier blasted Glenn's words with his definitive statement. His words set the testimony of Hughes's aides, as well as others, on end. Meier told me he had more details to add, but he wanted to be certain that I had a book deal before he would provide the information as he didn't intend to waste his time if the full story wasn't going to be made public.

Meier suggested I make every effort to locate Howard Eckersley as, "He knows a lot about Hughes being out of the Desert Inn."

He added, "I think he would talk to me about it if I called him. We did a lot together."

John Meier has reported in the past that he first met Howard Hughes in 1956 at the request of Noah Dietrich. This information is contained in a book written about Meier entitled *Age of Secrets*. There is no information in the book about Hughes being away from the Desert Inn. Meier had met Dietrich through some business dealings. He states he was personally assigned special projects by Hughes. This fit into Hughes's pattern of clandestine dealings. Meier says that Hughes personally called him in 1959 while Meier was in New York and convinced him to come to California. He met with Hughes several times at the Beverly Hills Hotel while in California. Meier officially went to work for Hughes Tool Company in 1966, and Hughes brought him to Las Vegas in 1967 as a scientific advisor and placed him in charge of trying to stop nuclear testing at the Nevada Test Site. Later, Hughes placed him in charge of mining acquisitions.

An interesting memo written by Hughes to Maheu in 1967 regarding the acquiring of mines was made public in Meier's book. It reads as follows: "Bob: You ask my advice as a friend. The only substantial loss involved here is to tie up some of these properties for our benefit. However, this may not be lost. We may perhaps be able to obtain an option on these properties if we work quickly enough tonight." This memo shows Hughes's direct interest in the mines and his advice to obtain options to insure they knew what they were buying before the deals were finalized.

Before long, Bob Maheu attempted to fire Meier for "certain indiscretions." Hughes vetoed the termination and wrote in a memo, "... I urge you not to fire Meier until we discuss him just a little more..." Meier was kept on until November 15, 1969, when he was pressured by Maheu to resign. Maheu later said, "Hughes requested that I go back to Mr. Meier and ask him to come back aboard forthwith." Maheu refused to bring him back. He argued that Meier caused too many problems. He had learned that Meier had no records of his mining acquisitions. He said he wasn't aware of who held the documents. Maheu was exasperated by this clear breach of business practice and believed Meier was hiding his far-reaching purchases of mining properties. He also learned that Bill Gay had approved some of the purchases even after Maheu had put a stop to the buying.

Bill Gay had vouched for Meier. This recommendation would have placed Meier in a very favorable light with Hughes, and he would have trusted Meier completely. But why was Hughes so set on keeping Meier on? Was there an underlying reason? Meier has said he worked directly for Hughes and not for Bob Maheu. Maheu contradicts this, but Hughes clearly had a special relationship with Meier as he encouraged Maheu to rehire the scientific advisor after he was forced to resign.

Meier has stated that he had "... ascended the rear stairway and met with Hughes in the Desert Inn penthouse." There were few who ascended the rear stairway. This was the secret passageway into the inner sanctum. It led to his boss who was holed up like some creature in a deep, dark cave. What did Meier do when he met with Hughes? My understanding of Hughes and his unique management style allows me to hypothesize. Surely, it involved mining acquisitions, and in all likelihood, Howard Eckersley was on duty when Meier climbed the fire stairwell. He seems to have been the gatekeeper who performed special assignments for Hughes. Of course, any of the aides would have let Meier in if ordered to do so by Hughes. Hughes ran his affairs very much the way the mob runs its operations. Often, the right hand didn't know what the left hand was doing. This allows the boss to compartmentalize his pursuits since he is the only one who controls the various operatives. This insures secrecy and his unfettered control.

Meier, in the past, has said Hughes insisted that he keep in constant contact with his aides and inform them of his movements. Meier said of the aides, "They were nurses. They took blood pressure, dressed him, took care of him, took care of his toilet habits. They didn't talk about him."

In 1971, Meier moved to New Mexico and ran unsuccessfully for the U.S. Senate. His past problems with the Summa kingpins came out and smothered his campaign. In March of 1972, Hughes Tool Company filed suit against Meier in order to recover money they claimed he had embezzled from Hughes in what they referred to as the "mining scam." By this time Hughes was deteriorating and may not have known about the legal actions.

I'm going to make a leap into the pool of speculation regarding John Meier. He is a man who always seems to be working the angles, trying to establish an advantage. Could it be that Meier was the first secret will caretaker for Hughes? According to Meier, while Hughes was staying in Vancouver, he tried to see him. I wondered, why did Hughes go to Vancouver? He met with LeVane Forsythe in Vancouver. Could Hughes have gone to Canada to see Meier as well? Hughes was there from March to September 1972. Meier moved to Vancouver in June of 1972. This would have given him three months to make the connection with Hughes in Vancouver.

If Meier was the first will caretaker, then he apparently attempted to deliver it to Joseph Fielding Smith, president of the Mormon Church, in Salt Lake City in July of 1972, but Smith had died. He passed away on July 2, 1972. The caretaker was in Salt Lake City and didn't know what to do with the will. In desperation, he anonymously called a Salt Lake City judge and asked him for advice. The judge would have been familiar with the handling of wills in Utah. The judge told him to keep the will until Hughes died. Now Meier was stuck with the will. He knew the hounds of the IRS were on his heels, and he would soon be a fugitive on the run. He had to rid himself of the priceless document.

When LeVane Forsythe met with Hughes in Vancouver in late August or early September of 1972, Hughes told him that someone else had held the will, but that person didn't want the responsibility any longer. Hughes passed the will to Forsythe, the new will holder. Forsythe also stated he received an anonymous call from a male, mentioning his code name Ventura, after taking possession of the will envelope. Forsythe was told to deliver the will to Melvin Dummar in Willard, Utah, after Hughes's death.

Meier has previously reported that he had obtained Hughes's personal papers from Mexican officials. The Hughes people left Acapulco in a panic when Hughes was dying, and the personal papers remained in Mexican police custody. The anonymous caller told Forsythe that he had some of Hughes's papers, and had figured out that Ventura was Forsythe and that he must have been the will caretaker.

In February of 1977, Forsythe received another call from a man using the alias Dan Harper. This may have been Meier as well. Harper told Forsythe that he needed to contact Melvin's attorney because Melvin had lied about not receiving the will. Remember that Meier couldn't come forward himself because he was a federal fugitive.

What was Meier's motivation for playing the role of puppeteer in the Mormon Will case? I'll take a chance and go for another lap in the pool of speculation. I believe it was an attempt to make a deal to have the charges against him dropped. When Meier met with attorney Harold Rhoden before the probate trial, he volunteered his cooperation. He said that he and Hughes had a deal where vast amounts of money were deposited in foreign banks for the purchase of mines. The mines didn't cost as much as expected, so the bank account balances were significant. Summa said Meier ended up with the money. He told Rhoden that he had witnesses and documentary evidence that Hughes had left the Desert Inn while living there. Remember that Edwin Daniel testified that Meier was with Hughes at the Mizpah Hotel. Rhoden had no power to make any kind of deal, so the negotiation fell through.

Meier was indicted for tax evasion in 1974, and he became a Canadian citizen in that year. In 1976 he was ordered in absentia by a U.S. court to repay Summa $7.9 million in restitution. He failed to do so and traveled the world, playing off his reputation and doing all kinds of deals with various people.

Meier was trapped outside of the United States. I believe he tried to affect the outcome of the trial by acting as master puppeteer by directing Forsythe from long distance. Why did he care? I believe it was for one of the oldest reasons in human existence—revenge. He wanted to see to it that Bill Gay and Summa (those who had turned on him) would lose everything.

I have speculated that Meier had been in touch with Forsythe. Could he have been in touch with Melvin as well? Melvin denies it, but where did Melvin get the idea of writing, "This was found by Joseph F. Smith's house in 1972. Thought you would be interested." Perhaps Meier called Melvin, using an alias, as he had done with Forsythe. Perhaps he told him he would receive a package and should take it to the Mormon Church and tell them it came from Joseph F. Smith's house as an explanation. This doesn't necessarily mean the will was a forgery, prepared and delivered by a trio of conspirators. I conjecture that this was Meier as the master puppeteer, moving the key players into position and coordinating their actions so that he could achieve his goal. He may have done it with the best of intentions.

I left a message for Meier, explaining my theories and requested his response if he had a problem with them. He has never responded.

In 1979, Meier was extradited to the U.S. and stood trial for obstruction of justice as a result of filing two false documents in the Hughes civil law suit. He was found guilty and sentenced to federal prison. He has always asserted a business associate named Robbie Roberts framed him. He was eventually transferred to a prison in British Columbia, Canada, and was paroled in January of 1981. In February of that year, Meier was indicted for the murder of a Vancouver stock promoter and business associate. He blames Roberts for these charges. The charges were negotiated down to harboring a fugitive.

It's my experience that serious charges are only negotiated down to nearly nothing because the government's case has unraveled and the original evidence has eroded. Meier pled no contest and was sent to prison again. He was released in September of 1983 at which time he returned to Canada.

When Rhoden met Meier in Canada before the probate trial in 1977, Meier informed him that Hughes had sneaked out of the Desert Inn to look at the Krupp Ranch and had traveled to Tonopah "on a few occasions."

Meier told me Hughes was at the Mizpah Hotel in Tonopah, Nevada. Hughes's director of engineering, Edwin Daniel, and mining consultant, Larry Smith, corroborate this. Daniel was at the bar when he saw a man and asked Meier, "... Is that who I think it is?"

There is a metal external fire escape staircase on the north side of the hotel. It provides access to the four floors of hotel rooms. It's logical to assume Meier and others traveled with Hughes to Tonopah in the dark and helped him climb the fire escape to gain access to his hotel room. This was the pattern set on numerous prior occasions.

Unfortunately, Meier has gone back on his word to me and will not return my calls, so we can't know exactly when this adventure happened, or where Hughes actually disappeared to, or what happened to him. I'm left to my own devices to answer this question.

A memo from Maheu dated March 16, 1968, informed Hughes that one of their employees, John Meier, "… had, in fact, obtained some options on, I believe, one specific property which included a lot of claims…" This proves Hughes was buying mines even before March 16, 1968. The Comstock mines were obtained on March 27, 1968. Maheu was surely referring to mines at the end of Howard's Road.

Meier has long contended that he had close dealings with President Richard Nixon's brother, Don. Maheu confirms this. Meier states that he was entangled in a web of conspiracies involving the Watergate burglary, bribes, and secret deals. He has been approached many times by the CIA, FBI, and other nations' intelligence agencies. He affirms that Robert Maheu was involved with various CIA projects, including the Jennifer Project.

In 1969, the CIA asked Hughes, through Maheu, to build the Glomar Explorer, a ship designed to appear as an underwater mining vessel when it was actually a deep-sea salvage vessel. One of the clandestine operations assigned to the special ship was the retrieval of a Soviet ballistic submarine that had sunk as a result of an accidental explosion in the deep blue waters of the Pacific. In 1974, seven hundred and fifty miles northwest of Hawaii, the salvage ship raised the sunken submarine SSBK- 129. The Hughes vessel had a huge claw attached amidships with a heavy duty hoisting mechanism. The claw was lowered sixteen thousand five hundred feet, and it grasped the damaged sub and brought it up inside the bowels of the ship. Eight Soviet submariners were found inside the sub and were honorably buried at sea.

U.S. authorities combed the sub for intelligence and techni-cal data in one of the many secret Cold War dramas that occurred in the shadows.

In his collaborative book, Meier confesses to coming from a family of clandestine operatives. His father served as a German infantryman in World War I. He came to the United States in 1920 and began his career as a German spy. In June 1942, a team of four German saboteurs landed by U-boat on Montauk Point, Long Island. Another team landed on Point Verdra Beach in Florida. Their dark mission was to blow up important rail lines and power systems in the U.S. The scheme was discovered, and the FBI manhunt was on. Meier has said his father hid two of the German saboteurs in his apartment on Long Island for a time, but he was never charged with any complicity in the conspiracy. Eventually they were captured, and six of the eight spies were executed.

When I last spoke with Meier, he asked for Melvin's tele-phone number, and I gave it to him. Melvin informed me that Meier called him and they had spoken. Meier, in a moment of remorse, told him he knew Dummar had told the truth about Hughes because Hughes had personally told Meier about being picked up by Melvin in the desert. This could have occurred on one of his visits to Hughes's pent-house after he ascended the staircase or one of their excur-sions into the outside world.

Sometimes evidence comes like a ghostly apparition in the night. A witness appears out of the fog and is able to clarify facts lost in time. I was working at my desk some years ago when I was notified of a visitor in the reception area of the Las Vegas FBI office. The walk-in visitor told the receptionist he had information about a murder. My partner and I went to meet the witness. He told us he had participated in a brutal murder of a lowlife loan shark who was putting pressure on him to pay a loan. He and two others had struck the loan shark several times in the head with a club. The blows were so ferocious the club broke. To finish the man they had stabbed him in the throat with the sharp edge of the broken club. The corpse had been rolled in a blanket like a swollen bratwurst and dumped in a ditch. The case was unsolved and was some years old. Now, the other murderers were threatening the witness, and he needed help from the FBI. His testimony solved the cold murder case as well as several others. We were able to assess the witness' story because we were familiar with the facts of the case and because we were available.

This time, a witness appeared because of a newspaper article. I had placed an ad in the Tonopah newspaper requesting anyone who had information about Howard Hughes to contact me. This lead was a dead end. Later, as fate would have it, Melvin granted an interview to a reporter for the *Lahontan Valley News* in Fallon, Nevada, in early April of 2004. Coincidently, the Associated Press picked up the story, and it ran in The *Las Vegas Review-Journal*. The next day, Melvin received a phone call from a man who told him a remarkable story. Melvin called me immediately and said, "This guy doesn't sound like the other wackos that have called me over the years. I think you should talk to him."

Every time I think I have a handle on this story, there's another twist, another turn, an amazing tale of intrigue. Not twenty minutes later, I heard from Guido Roberto Deiro. He called because he had read the AP newspaper article and had been struck by one statement. "It was 11 P.M., and Dummar said he had just passed the Cottontail Ranch brothel at Lida Junction where he pulled over to go to the bathroom." He told me the statement had hit him like a thunderbolt. Compassion for Dummar overwhelmed Deiro, and he knew he had knowledge that could help him.

Deiro provided detailed background on himself and gave me several references to his veracity and reliability. I subsequently checked him out. I found his credentials to be good.

Deiro said he had been associated with Ralph Englestad, the owner of the Imperial Palace Casino and Hotel in approximately 1965, when Englestad had purchased the then-bankrupt Thunderbird Field in North Las Vegas. Deiro was twenty-seven years of age at the time and held an airline transport license. He was rated for commercial, fixed wing, land, and seaplanes as well as helicopters. Englestad asked Deiro to manage the airport, and he was put in charge of promotions and advertising. The small, municipal airport began to be successful under his direction. Deiro was single and lived in the Skyrider Inn Motel on the airport property. The executive offices for the airport were also located in the motel. Deiro said, "One day, probably in late 1966, people from Hughes Tool Company came and looked at the operation and subsequently bought the airport." A man named John Seymour (now deceased) was placed over Hughes Airport Operations and was Deiro's superior.

Before long, Deiro was given the title of administrative assistant, and he began getting all kinds of strange assignments from the Hughes people. He was assigned the duty of "... entertaining and the care and feeding..." of business people associated with Hughes. He spent time with William Randolph Hearst Jr. and others. Then his title was changed to "facilitator." He informed me the assignments from the Hughes people became "more bizarre." On one occasion, he was instructed to go to a local car dealership after closing time and buy $1.5 million worth of cars for Hughes Tool Company. He said happily, "I got a 1967 new Ford Thunderbird out of the deal."

After a time he began receiving calls from Hughes's aide, Howard Eckersley. "He would connect me with Howard Hughes, and we'd talk airplanes and flying. He loved it." Then Deiro began receiving assignments to "... fly airplanes all over the place. I did instrument readings on approaches to various landing sites, dry lake beds, all over the place." Deiro explained that Hughes was interested in all kinds of subjects and he had an opinion about everything. Hughes expressed a mistrust of Blacks, Jews, and Italians and convinced Deiro to change his name from Guido Roberto Deiro to G. Robert Deiro. That way he wouldn't be viewed as an old world Italian. Hughes preferred to call him Bob.

Sometimes Hughes would send a Hollywood cinematographer with him, and they would film the approaches and departures to imaginary supersonic terminals. The films would be developed at Hughes headquarters on Romaine Street in Los Angeles and then delivered to Hughes in Las Vegas. He would study them and make new assignments for the next flying foray. Deiro believes Hughes was living vicariously through the films. Hughes told him he was interested in building a supersonic jet terminal (SST) somewhere near Las Vegas, and many of the flight patterns were part of the research for the SST project.

"Then the real strange stuff started. I would receive assignments to fly all over the place to inspect airplanes owned by Hughes. The planes had been parked for years. Some even had birds' nests in the engines. I would fly in and assess the condition of the planes and have the necessary repairs made and then fly them to another location."

"Howard Eckersley was Hughes's right hand man. He would call me and say, 'Have a plane fueled and ready at such and such a time. Be ready to depart at such and such a time. There will be one passenger. Don't file any flight plans.'" Deiro said these assignments were always at night. Deiro would have the plane ready and a black Chrysler sedan, usually driven by Eckersley, would arrive on the airport ramp at the appointed time. Hughes would get out and climb in the plane. In 1967, the airport had no control tower to report to and was deserted after dark. Deiro would be given the destination by Hughes. Usually they would fly a Cessna 310. Coincidently, this is the same type of plane Harold Rhoden lost his life in. It's a two-engine job, with a top speed of two hundred and fifty miles per hour. The two would fly to various proposed SST locations and talk flying. Sometimes Hughes took the wheel, but he was confident in Deiro's flying ability so he allowed him to make all the instrument approaches. As a facilitator, Deiro was personally directed by Hughes to establish heliports at seven locations in Las Vegas. One was at the Clark County Sheriff's Office. Others were at hospitals and Hughes's hotels, including the Desert Inn. Hughes instructed Deiro to induce the city of Las Vegas Police Department to acquire the first Nevada heliport. Deiro reported directly to Hughes on this project.

Deiro had been running "moonlight specials" on the side. He described these as advertised flights to brothels from the North Las Vegas Airport. Deiro described himself as a "single, twenty-eight-year-old pilot with a wild streak." He had his hands in all kinds of things. The Hughes people were aware of this, so one day he got a call from Eckersley and was told to get the plane ready. When Hughes arrived, Deiro was instructed to, "Fly me to a whorehouse." This occurred sometime in the late summer or early fall of 1967. He flew him to a cathouse in Ash Meadows, near Devil's Hole, located over the mountains about a hundred miles northwest of Las Vegas. It was called the Ash Meadows Ranch. The place is now closed.

Deiro flew customers to this house of ill repute regularly. He even ferried some of the hookers to Las Vegas where they caught flights to their home states. The girls worked two weeks on and two weeks off. Many of the ladies were call girls in Los Angeles, San Francisco, and other places who had left town for various reasons and found the safety of the legal brothels appealing. Then in November of 1967, he flew Hughes to the newly opened Cottontail Ranch brothel. The pilot explained that the bordello opened that same month. He had called ahead, and they knew he would arrive at a specific time so they had the truck ready to light up the runway by parking at the approach with the high beams on.

A month or so later, Deiro and Hughes flew to the brothel again. Deiro is sure it was during the holiday season in the winter of 1967, after Christmas and before New Year's Eve. This time he was flying a white Cessna 206. The plane made a low roll toward Gold Point then turned north. The moonless night was black except for the glow of Christmas lights on the front door of the ranch. The headlights of the truck illuminated the dirt runway at the far end of the airstrip. Guido Deiro dropped to four hundred feet and began his descending approach. He throttled down to seventy miles an hour as he passed over the truck. The wings wobbled slightly, but he was well within control. The landing was a difficult one but within his ability. He held the plane steady, knowing the aircraft would stall at sixty-five miles an hour.

At that point the plane should touch the ground. The Cessna 206 is a workhorse. Its top speed is one hundred and sixty miles per hour, and it is a single engine bush plane. It's perfectly designed for landing on dirt. The landing was relatively smooth, and the plane came to a stop after rolling four hundred feet. Deiro and his passenger got out and walked to the white building in the silent, moonless night, the headlights of the truck showing the way.

New Yorker Madam Beverly Harrell ran the place. She knew Deiro was coming, but she wasn't told about Hughes. The Cottontail people never were told who the scraggly old man was. At the time the Cottontail was three or four mobile homes connected together. Neither man wore a jacket because they were only outside for a brief time. Deiro said Hughes always wore the same clothes and dressed like a bum. On that night he wore a long sleeved shirt and old style gabardine pleated trousers that were too large for his thin frame. Deiro noted that Hughes's belt was cinched up tight in the third belt notch. He wore low cut white canvas deck shoes and white socks. The clothes had been worn many times as there was a distinct body odor to them. Hughes also had long gray-brown hair that fell to his shoulders and several days' growth of beard. Deiro said that Hughes carried what he described as a black leather doctor's bag with him. Hughes referred to it as his "possibles" kit. It contained sexual implements that Hughes required and may have contained drugs. He described Hughes's speech as rapid; he changed thoughts quickly, had wide mood swings, and seemed stimulated when he saw him.

They walked into the entry area and Deiro rang the doorbell. They were ushered in to the reception area and a line up was held. This is where the girls parade before the customer like in a horse auction, and where the patron picks his filly. There were only three or four girls in the stable as it was the holidays. In those days, the ladies wore their most luxurious gowns in the line-up. Like any salesperson, they advertised their wares.

Hughes chose a woman with a diamond imbedded in her left incisor. She was the same prostitute he had selected at Ash Meadows and the last time at the Cottontail. She had moved to the newly opened facility, hoping business would be better there. Hughes said he liked her because she was well-spoken and "She had class." Deiro said Diamond Tooth, who went by the name Sunny, was an elegant woman in her thirties from Minneapolis. Deiro went to the bar. He was expected to pay for his own drinks and entertainment. Hughes took care of his expenses and accompanied Diamond Tooth to her room.

Deiro said the small bar was managed by a woman who was referred to as the maid and there was a male bartender serving drinks. He also served as the bouncer. At the time, Deiro drank Johnny Walker Black Label. He bought required drinks for his date. They sat in some easy chairs, and he fed the jukebox.

There were at least two other male patrons at the bar. He can't recall anything about them. He doesn't know how many men may have been with girls in their rooms. He said he relaxed and told flying stories and listened to tunes while he waited for perhaps an hour or two, but Hughes didn't return. It was late, and Deiro was very tired and realized he had had one too many Johnny Walkers. He needed a nap before he could fly back to Las Vegas.

He recalls the time to be somewhere around 9 or 10 P.M. He was given permission by Beverly Harrell to lie down in a banquette in the kitchen and take a nap. They couldn't have him sleeping out in public. The place wasn't some flophouse. This was a well run enterprise, fueled by money. He said there was an egg timer for each girl on the kitchen counter, and when it went off, the patron's time was up. The girls would meet with the customer and negotiate a price, then they would go to the kitchen and deposit the money and set the timer for the allotted time. The girls came in during the long night and deposited their money in their locked mailboxes. Between the ringing egg timers and the movement of the girls, he woke up several times, but he slept hard between the interruptions.

At about 5:00 A.M., Deiro was awakened by the maid who told him he had to leave as all the girls had gone to bed because the house was closed until noon that day. She explained, "The girls need to rest." He asked for his friend and was told, "Your friend left."

"Where did he go?" He asked.

She responded, "I don't know."

"Well, when did he leave?"

She reported matter of factly, "A long time ago."

Deiro insisted that they check Sunny's room, but he was rebuffed. Even so, he explained he wasn't very concerned because, if his memory is accurate, he was told that Hughes had left with someone. He doesn't recall who it was. He explained he was more concerned about the possible loss of his job.

Deiro took off in the Cessna as the sun was breaking in the east. He circled the area a few times gaining altitude, but he didn't see Hughes wandering in the desert. He wasn't aware that Howard's Road cut through the desert below him, dissecting it like a faded scar. The desert below was barren and featureless in every direction. As a good-bye, he buzzed the brothel while laughing to himself as he knew the noise would stir those inside. Then he flew down the highway for an hour or so until he touched down on runway seven in North Las Vegas.

Deiro didn't know what to think about Hughes disappearing, but he never heard a word about the incident. It turned out to be the last time Hughes spoke with him or flew with him. Deiro says he didn't think much about the cold shoulder because most everything he had done for Hughes was strange and out of the ordinary. He felt, "No news was good news."

There is an undated memorandum, in which Hughes writes, in part, "... I prefer the new place and I have reason to believe there will be no repetition of the Desert Inn episode. Of course, I am not sure. But I have taken steps." Deiro believes his memo refers to the Cottontail Ranch, and that perhaps Hughes had found another brothel after the fiasco where Hughes had to find his way back into the security of the Desert Inn.

Deiro told me Hughes had an office not far from the rear of the Sands Hotel. The office was set up for Nadine Henley when she visited Las Vegas. The office was in a converted two thousand square foot white brick house. Deiro has been to this location many times, and he believes Hughes asked Melvin to drop him off at the rear of the Sands so he could make his way to the office and make contact with his aides.

I found Deiro's report to be solid because I was able to judge his information under the microscope of what I knew the facts to be. It was a good fit. Even though Deiro had missed connections with Hughes at the brothel, he continued to work for Hughes Tool Company at Alamo Airways, located at McCarran International Airport in Las Vegas. His office was moved to that facility. He established a training center at Alamo and was appointed director of aviation facilities. He was extremely busy with these responsibilities but continued to entertain various people for the Hughes Tool Company. Deiro told me, "I could see storm clouds on the horizon. Maheu was expanding his hold on many of Hughes's operations, and the true powers were troubled by it." Eckersley was Deiro's conduit to Hughes, and he informed the aide that he wanted to marry Joan Calhoun, a secretary at the Desert Inn, and therefore couldn't continue with his twenty-four-seven lifestyle. Before long, Eckersley set up an appointment with Hughes's long time millionaire pal, C. Arnold Smith. He was a high profile businessman with whom President Richard Nixon spent election eve.

In approximately June of 1968, Deiro went to work for Smith's Golden West Airlines as vice president of administration. He also was appointed vice president of United States National Bank in California. He is convinced that Hughes set up both jobs for him. Before he left Las Vegas, John Seymour sat down with Deiro and "amended" his flight logs. In other words, they erased all references to Hughes and any special flights. Deiro was instructed to sign a nondisclosure agreement that prohibited him from discussing any Hughes Tool Company business. Seymour also took control of the file cabinets and records for Thunderbird Field. Hughes had given Deiro a leather pilot's bag with the initials HRH to show his appreciation for his efforts. Deiro later sold it at auction for nearly nothing.

Deiro told me he knew John Meier and had flown him and other mining people to Tonopah and other locations after the Cottontail incident. He recalls that on one trip an attorney from Houston was with Meier and Clarence Hall looking at mines.

Now, the memo from Hughes dated December 30, 1967 makes complete sense. The memorandum read, "Make sure please we have the Houston firm's promise of secrecy. From everyone! Tell him again at the end, and tell him I have additional property to acquire in that area and any leakage of these plans - boom - impossible."

Deiro also admitted personally knowing Robert Maheu, and to this day maintains a social relationship with him, but he has never told him about his contact with Hughes, nor have they discussed the affairs of the Hughes Tool Company. He explained, "That's just the way it is with former Hughes employees." Deiro was required to sign a disclaimer when he was hired by Summa. He was not to discuss his job or assignments with anyone. He has honored this commitment until now.

Helen Holland, a lovely grandmother, had been working as the secretary for the commanding general at Hill Air Force Base in Utah when she was hired by Deiro in 1967. She was his personal secretary and handled all correspondence and required paper work for Nevada Airport operations. She told me she personally took dictation from Howard Hughes in late 1967 or early 1968. He dictated memoranda regarding the operation of the airport and aircraft. She often transferred Hughes's telephone calls to Deiro. She was aware that Hughes and Deiro had contact with each other, but she didn't know the details. She also told me Howard Eckersley came to the airport executive offices with some paperwork several times and discussed the documents that were sent by Hughes. She explained the qualities most required by the Hughes Company were competence, keeping operations quiet, and being discreet. In other words, what is done inside Hughes Tool Company stayed inside Hughes. She remained as a trusted secretary to other Hughes executives after Deiro left.

Deiro informed me he was approached by the CIA sometime in 1970. The agency flew him and his wife to Washington, D.C. and laid out the red carpet to entice him to become involved in the management of Omni International, a charter airline company functioning for the CIA in Zaire, Africa. He took a battery of tests and was cleared to go to Africa, but Joan nixed the deal. He is sure Hughes had something to do with this affair as he had close ties to the Nixon administration and CIA.

Some may have a problem with the fact that Deiro says he didn't know about Melvin picking up Hughes near the Cottontail Ranch. The probate trial publicity was far-reaching and intense. He surely would have heard about it. As I reviewed much of the newspaper coverage of the trial at the time, it became evident that although the trial received a great deal of publicity, there wasn't significant reporting about the pickup site being near the Cottontail Ranch. Nor was there much said about Hughes's aides adamantly denying that Hughes had left the Desert Inn. Apparently, there was nothing that triggered his memory about the event. Deiro told me he just didn't give it much thought at the time. He never saw the movie, *Melvin and Howard,* and was extremely busy in 1977 while working as a shift boss in the Holiday Casino, running a flight school, and starting a real estate auction company. He said he didn't pay much attention to the trial and read very little about it. He considered Dummar a fool, and his understanding was that Melvin had reported finding an old man at his gas station in northern

Nevada. He never associated Dummar with the Cottontail Ranch. None of the publicity he was aware of rang any bells in his head. He had essentially written Melvin off as a nut. He said he had great interest in the defamation lawsuit between Hughes and Bob Maheu because he knew both men. When he read the Associated Press article mentioning the Cottontail, it rang a bell and brought a flood of memories back. He told me he had recently lain awake reconstructing the events in his mind. He now considers this his personal crusade for the sake of justice.

I'm sure there are those whose probable explanation for Deiro's awakening is that when the probate trial publicity was fully intense, Deiro was reluctant to become involved. He didn't want the attention or the headaches that testifying would bring. He was married and had children and was a respected member of the community, and he may not have wanted his youthful indiscretions exposed in public. He laid low, hoping justice would prevail and Melvin would get what was rightfully his. It didn't work that way. After all these years, Deiro read the newspaper article about Melvin and maybe his conscience bit him. There will be those who believe he decided to make up for the past by telling his story now. But it can also be true that the passage of time sometimes enables the truth, as old restraints vanish with time.

Why would Deiro come up front after all this time? He has been involved in the gaming industry and real estate in Las Vegas for many years. He has held responsible business positions. He is a former reserve police officer and just recently resigned as foreman of the Clark County Grand Jury. His life has changed since those heady days as a single, swashbuckling pilot, but he continues to hold numerous

242

pilot certifications although his flying days are essentially over. He has served the community as a former member of the Clark County Water District – Citizen's Advisory Council on Underground Water Management. He has been named Las Vegas Citizen of the Month for his charitable work, and he even has a street named after him. It's called "Count Deiro Drive," in honor of Deiro's father who was an Italian count, which makes Deiro a count by birth. He is a very successful man. He isn't the kind of person who would concoct such a remarkable story. He has nothing to gain and has asked for nothing in return for his disclosure to me or anyone else. The secrecy of Deiro's assignments and the compartmentalization of tasks certainly fit with Hughes's "MO." Deiro told me, "To tell you the truth, there's nothing in this for me but possible recrimination." Plus, he contradicts his friend Robert Maheu's opinion that Hughes never left the Desert Inn.

He told me emphatically, "Dummar is telling the truth. I feel so sorry that I didn't put the facts together at the time of the trial and come forward." Deiro wants to make things right by telling the truth about Hughes. He admits he can't get Melvin the money Hughes willed him, but he can repair history and restore Melvin's reputation. I believe he's telling the truth.

Now Hughes's memo about Eckersley presented during the trial makes complete sense. In part, it read, "... I feel better doing something highly secret like this when Howard was on and it is at night..." Eckersley was Hughes's secret facilitator. He set up Hughes's trips with Deiro.

Eckersley lied when he testified that he didn't know what the memo was referring to. He compounded his crime when he was asked, under oath, "... You clearly recall that on every night from December twenty-eighth to the thirty-first, from seven P.M. to three A.M., Mr. Hughes was in the Desert Inn and not out in the desert somewhere getting a ride back to Las Vegas?"

He answered curtly, "That is correct."

The fact is, now I had another witness with direct evidence that Hughes left the Desert Inn. I had evidence that he was at the Cottontail on or near the day Melvin rescued him. And I had corroboration of Melvin's improbable description of the richest man in America in 1967.

The Cottontail Ranch has a new master of the house. Mo Lospinoso, also known as Mo Greene, who bought the place in August of 2003. He has been engaged in the Hollywood movie industry for several years and purchased the brothel "for entertainment." I spoke with Mo after Deiro provided his story. Mo gave me a rundown on the history of prostitution in Esmeralda County. He said, at the height of Goldfield's boom days, there were as many as one thousand eight hundred ladies of the night working their trade. That was one for every ten residents during Goldfield's heyday. The ladies were viewed as "society women" in the land of rough miners. Some of the early black-and-white photos displayed in the courthouse show well-dressed ladies with parasols strolling down the sidewalks of Goldfield. These women were prostitutes.

Mo told me he had heard of the infamous Diamond Tooth and believed she used the name "Sunny." He had no idea if she was still alive or where she might be. He explained that "his girls" come from all over the country. He even has a girl from Belgium working at his place. They all come for one thing—money. Many are divorced or come from broken homes or abusive fathers or husbands. Some enjoy their work, but money drives them all. Mo wasn't aware that Howard Hughes had visited his establishment, but he had heard rumors of Hughes's shadow life. He was aware Hughes was an awkward introvert and used his money and power to get what he wanted. Mo said he was also aware that Madam Beverly Harrell often used a truck to light up the bordello's airstrip for incoming planes when she ran the place. Now, the brothel has been closed down again. Mo has had some financially related difficulties, and the county has pulled his license.

The Esmeralda Sheriff's Office keeps track of the prostitutes plying their trade in the county. The girls must register and are required to have weekly physicals to check for AIDs or venereal disease. Unfortunately their records don't go beyond 1980. The saga of Diamond Tooth will have to remain a mystery.

I personally disagree with prostitution as a lifestyle. It's seldom a victimless crime. In all cases, the victim is the hooker as she gives up her body to unloving men. The woman is dehumanized and becomes nothing more than a sexual object, a breathing sex toy. But I'm aware that many street hookers are severely mistreated and abused by pimps and johns and held captive by drug addiction. I've seen women with black eyes and severe welts from being beaten with coat hangers by their pimps. At least, working in a regulated brothel provides them protection in a drug-free environment.

Legalized prostitution is currently under assault in some counties of Nevada. In the past it was accepted as long as it was kept in the shadows; a dark secret hidden from polite society. Now the industry is more aggressive, pushing the envelope. Gaudy billboards line the main streets. Pictures of partially naked women are an in-your-face reminder of

Nevada's dirty little secret. The brothels are no longer out of sight and out of mind.

When the notorious Madam, Beverly Harrell, passed away in 1995, many secrets were buried with her. The names of famous customers, secret political intrigues, and unusual happenings were interred with her body. She was originally from New York but moved to California, and finally to Goldfield. She was politically active and even ran for the Nevada legislature, which she lost by only 17 votes.

On a hunch, I pursued Harrell's husband, hoping he was still alive. Howard Harrell has left western Nevada behind and lives as a contented recluse in the thick pine mountains of California. When I finally caught up with him, I found him residing in a single wide mobile home away from brothels, prostitutes, and the heat of the desert. Now, he has a small circle of friends, and he told me he has tried to push "the old days" out of his mind. Harrell is a congenial seventy-seven-year-old who seems satisfied with what life has brought him. I asked, "When did you open the Cottontail Ranch?"

He responded, matter of factly, "A long time ago. It was in November of 1967. Beverly was the owner. It was her idea to open the place. She made all the decisions. We moved to Goldfield from southern California, but I didn't spend much time at the place in the beginning. I lived in Las Vegas and dealt cards in a casino for a while."

I asked him if he recalled an old, longhaired man visiting the brothel in November and December of 1967. He said no. I asked if he remembered a working girl named Sunny who had a diamond in her front tooth.

He said no, then added, "There was a maintenance man and a housekeeper (both deceased) who worked for Beverly in the beginning." He said that, "They also ran the bar. I wasn't there regularly until later. I finally sold the place in 2001."

I had struck out in my attempt to corroborate details provided by Deiro, but I gave it one more shot. "Have you ever heard of Howard Hughes visiting the Cottontail?" I asked.

There was a momentary silence. Then he made me smile when he reported, "Beverly told me Hughes had been there more than once."

I immediately jumped on his assertion. "What exactly did she say about it? When was he there?"

He said, hesitatingly, "She just told me she had seen him there, but she didn't give any details." I savored the moment, then he continued, "Beverly wanted to go to the authorities about it. She wanted to go to the cops in Las Vegas and tell the story about Hughes when we heard about the trial, but I talked her out of it. I told her it would bring her nothing but trouble. There were too many powerful people involved, and I thought she would be in danger."

I said, "You know, Melvin Dummar said he picked up Hughes south of the Cottontail."

Harrell responded, "Yeah, there's a road six miles south of there. They sure did a job on Dummar."

I asked him, "Why didn't Beverly come forward during the trial in Las Vegas?"

His answer was immediate, "She didn't want that kind of trouble. I mean, she was always looking for publicity, but that was dangerous publicity."

After talking with Harrell, the first thought that came to mind was, Why didn't the proponents of the will pursue this investigative angle and depose Beverly Harrell about the possibility of Hughes being at her place as he was found in the vicinity of the only civilization for miles—the Cottontail Ranch?

The key to establishing the reliability of a witness is corroboration of the information provided by the witness. I have multiple corroboration for Hughes being out of the Desert Inn. Edwin Daniel, John Henderson, Doctor Ford, Larry Smith, Robert Deiro, John Meier, Melvin, and now Harrell, all said he was out of the hotel. The room records show no activity by the aides from December twenty-sixth to the thirtieth. If they weren't home, then Hughes wasn't home. He wouldn't be able to function without them. And I had deed records showing Hughes had options to buy mines at the end of Howard's Road.

How did Hughes end up on Howard's Road after he left the Cottontail Ranch? This is a missing link in the investigative chain. I rolled this question over in my mind and let it marinate for a while. Deiro states that he last saw Hughes about nine or ten o'clock. The old man may have been high on a drug, and he had his own expense money. Would it be possible that Hughes had a conflict with Diamond Tooth or an altercation with someone else at the brothel? He was accustomed to getting his way. He was demanding and rude by nature. Maybe the bouncer pushed him out the door. It's believed no one at the Cottontail knew who he was. It wouldn't be the first time someone had been thrown out of a whorehouse.

The last time he was there, perhaps a patron, maybe someone from the bar, followed the old man outside. Hughes didn't know what had become of Deiro, and he couldn't go back inside to ask, so he was stuck outside in the cold parking lot. Where would he go? What would he do?

He would certainly accept a ride offered by someone exiting the building. He didn't have any other options. Perhaps he was driven down the highway, and the driver pulled off the road and robbed him. Maybe the "possibles bag" was taken from him. We know he didn't have any money when Melvin picked him up because he asked Melvin for his spare change. Also, the bag wasn't with him. Maybe he was slugged in the side of the head and pushed out. Perhaps the feeble old man fell to the ground and lay there helpless and bleeding.

Another possibility is that a passing motorist picked up Hughes and robbed him. Or, perhaps, he walked in the desert for seven and a half miles. This alternative is doubtful as he wouldn't have had the strength to make such a trek. A final option is that he was picked up by someone he knew, but then why would he have been dumped in the desert?

Perhaps Hughes and Deiro were at the Cottontail on the twenty-seventh or twenty-eighth, and maybe Hughes was picked up by Meier and taken to Tonopah, then disappeared again on the twenty-ninth while attempting to scout the mines on his own near Howard's Road where he was rescued by Melvin. Of course, it's possible that Hughes went missing more than once. Meier has said Hughes was out of the Desert Inn, "… on a few occasions." The evidence certainly bears this out.

The thirty-day option to buy mines at the end of Howard's Road ran from approximately December 24, 1967 through January 24, 1968, so if Hughes was going to scout these mines it would only make sense for him to do so before the purchase was finalized on January twenty-fourth. It would have taken him some time to recuperate from his disastrous adventure at the Cottontail, but perhaps two weeks or so later, he made another surreptitious journey. This time, he went to Tonopah. We know John Meier and Edwin Daniel saw him there.

Daniel said he was there with some mining people, including John Meier. Meier confirms this. Daniel saw Hughes in the Mizpah Hotel, and the next morning, ... "there was a certain amount of excitement in the lobby..." He went on to say that Meier had told him, "... the old man is lost..." We know John Henderson saw him at American Flat. Hughes was walking alone on a road toward some abandoned mines.

We can infer that since Hughes was with mining people in Tonopah, he wasn't "lost" as they believed. He was, presumably, out looking at mines. If this occurred in mid-January 1968, which mining properties did he own at that time? Only the thirty-two mines at the end of the ranch road.

The sliver of Meier continues to stick in my foot. I would know the complete story if he had continued to cooperate, but that is water under the bridge. In any event, I now know that Hughes was at the Cottontail Ranch and ended up on Howard's Road where he was rescued by Melvin.

Epilogue

This has been a tale of two men. One is ordinary, a regular Joe, an underdog. The other was an uncommon man of great achievement. These two men's lives collided for a moment in time in the dark clutches of the Nevada desert, but the repercussions of this brief connection continue to this day. Melvin has been maligned for years because he told the remarkable, unimaginable truth.

I began this journey as a skeptic but finished as an advocate. Throughout this endeavor I have had the nagging concern that Melvin's health wouldn't allow him to survive the long protracted process of investigation and publicity. This concern was always in my mind, like a recurring dread. When the job was finally concluded, I called and reported my findings to Melvin and told him his story would assuredly become public. I explained in detail that the evidence was conclusive in his favor.

There was a long silence on the other end of the line.

Then he exclaimed, "Thank God! I've suffered in silence for over twenty-five years. Everyone I meet, when they learn who I am, looks at me like I'm some sort of freak. Now, after all this time, I can finally hold my head up. I feel great about it. I'm vindicated. I love it!"

I was pleased with his response. It had been a long journey. Unfortunately, it was too late for justice, but now belatedly, Melvin had been justified. I exclaimed sincerely, "I'm glad it came out the right way for you."

"I'm very happy. It shows I was telling the truth all along. I was scorned, sick, and nearly broke. The court was rigged against me. As God is my witness, I found Mr. Hughes in the desert. I don't know about the will being his, but this changes everything for me. Thanks." Melvin responded.

He had found himself on a magic carpet ride when the will surfaced, but the rug was pulled out from under him. He was stabbed with the daggers of accusation and bludgeoned with the title of fool. He was made to carry this heavy burden for so many years. I was impressed by the fact that in spite of it all, he was still standing, and now the world would know the truth.

When I first stood on Howard's Road, a dust devil danced its way across the desert in the distance. It sucked up the loose sand from the desert floor and spun it around in a funnel shaped swirl. I wondered if agreeing to do some investigation on a thirty-five-year-old case would be like chasing that dust devil. In many ways it was, but in the end, it was worth it.

Howard Hughes was an enigma. He was a secretive, self-absorbed man of great ability and immense wealth, and yet, he was chased by his own demons throughout his whole life. In spite of this he believed he was in control. He once bragged, "I can buy any man in the world." He surrounded himself with people who evolved into piranhas that fed off the flesh of his fortune. He was a man driven by obsession, by phobias, and by genius. In spite of his genius, he may have written the most bewildering will in history.

His empire was vast, and his aides helped isolate him, particularly near the end of his life. They contributed to the secrecy that surrounded him. Hughes was often tyrannical in his style, and his inner circle of subordinates treated him like a king. His demons began to devour him, causing his descent into a dark mental abyss in the mid-1960s. His physical condition deteriorated simultaneously, and he was allowed to crawl into a prison of his own making, eventually to die, much like the lunatics of the Middle Ages who were put in dungeons. The difference was that his dungeons were luxurious hotel suites all over the world.

Hughes's key men, those who ran his companies, were interested in expanding his holdings and making more money. They left the personal care of their boss to underlings who were ill equipped to do so. The Mob lives by the absolute code of "omerta." Like the Mob, this code of silence also applied to those inside the Hughes organization. Everyone followed the party line and refused to cooperate with people on the outside. They kept operations quiet and were discreet in the extreme. Their power grew as Hughes faded, and eventually, Hughes became an irrelevant irritant they learned to work around.

The so-called executive assistants, his aides, were the gatekeepers, the palace guards, Howard Hughes's outer skin, who jealously exercised their power. They had been promoted from menial jobs to the care and handling of the emperor. I contend that many of them were promoted not because of great aptitude, but because they followed orders no matter how absurd they may have been. They've been described by others as worms and zombies. I prefer to call many of them eunuchs, as they were completely emasculated by fear of losing their substantial salaries and power.

Some of them provided contradictory testimony and perjured themselves during the trial, and as such, it's difficult to know when they were lying or when they were telling the truth. They all testified that they were ordered to keep meticulous logs of every occurrence during their shifts, including when Hughes went to the bathroom, how long it took, what he ate, and how long it took him to eat. The logs were of such vital importance that as soon as there was a hint of trouble, they were immediately destroyed. Potentially valuable evidence was shredded and burned.

Hughes attempted to buy Las Vegas and made every effort to tie up the gold and silver reserves of Nevada. Hughes Tool Company made three mining claim purchases in late 1967 and early 1968. Each claim included numerous mines. They were the properties at the end of Howard's Road, the Comstock Mines at American Flat, and the Good Springs mines in Clark County. These were, in the words of Robert Maheu, "... a couple or three properties we thought were good acquisitions." These acquisitions were secured by options to buy, thirty days prior to the actual title transfers.

The thirty-two mines at the end of Howard's Road were held by option on December 29, 1967. Hughes was the de facto owner of these properties when he was found on Howard's Road by Melvin. The second purchase of mines was made on March 27, 1968, near American Flat. An eyewitness put Hughes at American Flat, walking on a dirt road near some mines. This witness reported a Chrysler parked nearby. Those who knew Hughes best verified that Hughes's corporation had Chryslers, and "… he liked them." In addition, Edwin Daniel put Hughes and some mining men at the Mizpah Hotel in Tonopah during this general time period when he asked, "Is that who I think it is?" He was obviously referring to Hughes. The next day the mining people were in a frenzy because Hughes had disappeared.

There was no public knowledge of these mines at the end of Howard's Road until my investigation discovered the deed in 2002. Hughes owned the mines at the end of that road, and he personally dealt with those mines. How would the evidence about the deed and Howard's Road have affected the outcome of the trial? Would it have been enough to corroborate Melvin's testimony? We'll never know, but I believe it would have tipped the scales toward the legitimacy of the will. This is certainly a case of "if only." Unfortunately, the rust of time has sealed many investigative doors. Many of the potential witnesses are dead, or have grown old and are in heaven's waiting room. Time has corroded the truth, but it may also have preserved unexpected facts.

When Melvin picked up Hughes and unquestionably saved his life, Hughes responded as anyone would. He wanted to reward the man who saved him. One-sixteenth of his estate was a pittance when you consider his vast wealth. This reward was perfectly reasonable for a man who knew he had been delivered from certain death.

Roy Crawford testified that he was on duty from December twenty-sixth through the thirtieth. He worked the 3:00 A.M. to 11:00 A.M. shift. There is no record of who worked the day shift. Howard Eckersley worked the same days on the 7:00 A.M. to 3:00 A.M. shift. Eckersley had experience whisking Hughes in and out of hotels without being detected. Added to this, the Desert Inn records showed no activity for the aides' suites from December twenty-seventh through the thirtieth. Where were the aides, and where was Hughes?

All of the aides were told by Hughes that he had a holographic will and that they were named "… by job description rather than by name." They were also told the will was being kept by someone Hughes trusted. This was consistent testimony provided by all the aides in the trial. The will was sloppy and filled with misspellings and overwritings. Several physicians testified and explained that these characteristics are common in individuals suffering from acute kidney disease.

The legitimate Hughes will would have had eight specific elements to it. Any will that doesn't conform to these elements could not be the actual will. These elements are: 1. The will was holographic. 2. It was written on yellow lined paper. 3. The employees were not named but were identified by job description. 4. The will was held by a trusted courier. 5. The will was written before 1970. (It should be recalled the Mormon Will was signed on March 19, 1968.) 6. Two weeks prior to his death Hughes said he had a holographic will. 7. Only Hughes had seen the will. 8. The will would be sloppily prepared and contain attentional errors.

I believe we can logically add a ninth element. There is a preponderance of evidence that Melvin rescued Hughes and saved his life, therefore, a will naming Melvin as a beneficiary would be a reasonable element. The Mormon Will incorporated all of these elements. It's the only one that does. Melvin must have been a wizard if he forged the will because no one outside the personal aides knew about these elements until the trial in 1977. These elements were organized and grouped by me in 2004.

Reporter Ray Friess told me that Kay Glenn panicked when he learned that Dr. Ford would testify that Glenn had said Hughes had been out of the Desert Inn. Glenn essentially admitted it was true. After the holidays, most of the aides probably went home for a few days, as Hughes demanded double shifts from his aides on all holidays. This was his way of testing their fealty and reassuring himself that he was more important than their own families. Eckersley and Crawford stayed behind and pulled their shifts. This provided them with a perfect opportunity for their surreptitious adventure.

Allegations of jury tampering have not been proven, but there is cause to believe it occurred. The jury unwisely relied on one man's typewritten notes, and after eight months of torturous testimony, they took the easy route and followed the leader. There were other serious violations of law and improprieties during the trial. There was perjury, destruction of evidence, and intimidation of witnesses. The matter of the Mormon Will did not get a fair and legal hearing.

The probate trial was a struggle for the Hughes empire and fortune. Participant witnesses and experts provided testimony. I wasn't present at the trial, so it's not possible for me to assess the witnesses. But from my research, it appears that the jury may have questioned Melvin's testimony because it was a wild tale told by a man who had lied in the past. Forsythe was found unreliable because only his deposition was read into the trial record, and his complete lack of attention to small details and evidence tampering tripped him up. Unfortunately you're stuck with the witnesses you have. You can't testify for them, and the chips will fall where they may.

Experts who had differing opinions debated the physical evidence, particularly the handwriting. The contestants' experts concentrated on the will and found it to be of poor quality, while the proponents' experts reviewed volumes of known handwriting and compared it to the will. The handwriting experts were basically discounted, as the two sides canceled each other out. In the end, the jury found the will to be illegitimate and, by inference, a forgery.

If the will was a forgery, then who forged it? The universities, the Hughes Medical Institute, The Church of Jesus Christ of Latter-day Saints, and the Boy Scouts can all be excluded for obvious reasons, and for the fact that they would not have known about Melvin Dummar, who was specifically named in the will. The ex-wives can also be eliminated for the same reason. The key men, personal aides, and Lummis can be eliminated because they fought against the will during the trial. We are left with Noah Dietrich, the executor, and Melvin Dummar, or someone associated with them.

It's very doubtful that Dietrich would have known about Dummar. That leaves Melvin, but no charges were ever brought against him. The Nevada Attorney General's Office focused on him, but after an extensive investigation, Nevada law enforcement authorities stated, "No grounds were found to prosecute him on any charges." The FBI didn't bring charges against anyone associated with the trial.

Maybe Melvin's wife wrote the will. If so, why would she misspell her own last name? How would she know about the institutions that Hughes respected that were named in the will? How would she know about William Lummis and both of Hughes's former wives? How could she know about Hughes's use of yellow lined paper? How could she have used the same brand of pen and ink formula that Hughes was known to have used during the pertinent time period? There were three thousand inks on the market at the time. The ink that was used in the will was last manufactured in 1972, four years before the will surfaced.

How would Bonnie know the Desert Inn had a Pitney Bowes postage meter? And how would she have stamped the will envelope with the meter showing a March, Las Vegas stamp for six cents? The cost of a stamp in 1968 (the year the will was signed) was six cents. The cost of a stamp in 1976, when the will was delivered, was thirteen cents. Logically, this only leaves one conclusion—Hughes wrote the will in 1968 when President McKay was leading the Mormon Church.

After a good deal of research, my investigation began with an interview of Melvin. I had no other evidence at that point in time. My old friend, the mobster, would have counseled me, "Forgit aboud it! You're rockin' a dead baby." It was an uphill climb, but my investigation proves that the baby isn't dead.

Melvin said he picked up an old man in the desert. He told several people about picking up a derelict who said he was Howard Hughes shortly after the incident occurred in 1967-68. If this were a conspiracy to get Hughes's money, Melvin would have required the foresight to set the stage nine years earlier by telling the story of the rescue in the desert to several acquaintances.

Melvin described Hughes as old and thin and over six feet tall. He had shoulder length hair and bled from what Melvin thought to be his left ear. This description has been verified by George Francom, Mell Stewart, Robert Deiro, and others. Melvin couldn't have known what Hughes looked like at the time or that Hughes had a potential bleeding problem from a nodule located just above the left ear.

Judge Hayes, a veteran jurist, was interviewed after the trial by a reporter and was questioned about his opinion of contradictory expert handwriting testimony. He said, "It was maddening to listen to these calligraphic mercenaries... It was stupefying." On another occasion he stated, "The verdict could have gone either way. I had made notes to myself in the event the jury came back for the proponents or the other side."

From the beginning of this endeavor, I hoped to find a new witness who could lay out the truth. As it turned out, I found three: John Meier, head of mining operations for Hughes, was possibly the original will holder. And he may have acted as puppeteer in an effort to support the Mormon Will. He has told me emphatically, "Howard Hughes was with me and others in the Tonopah area. We were looking at mines. He went out on his own and got lost." It would be difficult to get a stronger statement of fact. He told attorney Rhoden that Hughes had been out of the Desert Inn, "on a few occasions." Unfortunately, his complete recitation of the facts are being held by him for some inexplicable reason. It appears that Hughes was with Meier, probably sometime after the Cottontail incident, and he went off by himself again. Did he go to look at the mines at the end of Howard's Road?

A brave man of integrity, Robert Deiro, came forward on his own with nothing to gain and settled the matter when he stated that Howard Eckersley had made arrangements for Hughes to be flown to the Cottontail Ranch brothel during the holiday season between Christmas and New Year's, 1967. Deiro ferried the old man to Lida Junction and took a nap at the cathouse. When he awakened, Hughes was gone.

He went on to describe what Hughes looked like and how he was dressed that night. Melvin's description of the man he rescued on December twenty-ninth fit to a tee.

Hughes wrote a memo during the Desert Inn period that stated in part, "... I feel better doing something highly secret like this when Howard was on duty and it is at night." Howard Eckersley was on duty from the twenty-sixth to the thirtieth. We can logically postulate that Hughes was carried down the nine floors of the fire stairwell by a minimum of four people, one holding each corner of the stretcher. Hughes didn't have the leg strength to climb the stairs on his own. The room service records indicated that the aides were out of the building during the pertinent time period.

I was lucky enough to dig up Howard Harrell. His information is considered hearsay, but he has no reason to be lying about the fact that his wife of many years told him Howard Hughes had been to the Cottontail. She felt so strongly about it that she wanted to go to the authorities and tell them. Harrell could certainly provide direct evidence about talking his wife out of divulging her information to the authorities.

Several witnesses testified that it was easily possible to "... go to the back door, and open it, and go down the stairs." Hughes would have left after dark, which was their pattern, probably late on the twenty-sixth. He was taken to the North Las Vegas Airport and delivered to Deiro by Eckersley.

Hughes had a history of frequenting prostitutes, and he may have had a problem inside the Cottontail as Deiro slept. He could have been picked up and thrown out of a car. Later that night, Melvin stumbled upon Hughes on Howard's Road and took him to Las Vegas. They would have arrived late on the twenty-ninth or early the thirtieth. By the time the Hughes associates learned that Hughes was safe in Las Vegas, and after picking up his abandoned car, it would have been later on the thirtieth. Then they returned to Las Vegas and their suites, and the pattern of phone calls and room service continued as usual on the thirty-first. This investigation had a very narrow focus. I had no interest in writing another biography of Hughes. Two pivotal questions were in my sights. Did Melvin pick up Howard Hughes in the desert? I believe there's solid evidence that, indeed, he did. The other question is: Did Hughes write the will? There is sufficient evidence to prove it was written by his own hand.

The world's perception of Melvin Dummar needs to change. He's been resented and vilified for years. He's been called a dunce, a fool, and a liar. Dummar is an ordinary guy, not perfect by any means, but he was minding his own business and doing his own thing when he fell into a cauldron of boiling water that he was not equipped to handle. He made mistakes, but he's not a fraud. Melvin was acting out the parable of the Good Samaritan by picking up an old man in need. This innocent act lit the fuse that eventually blew up in his face and has affected his life ever since.

The biggest losers in this whole episode were Melvin and the fine institutions and charities that should have received what Hughes willed them. History has been repaired, but can there ever be restitution of justice? Society owes Melvin an apology. There is also a great deal of money owed him and the other beneficiaries.

Harold Rhoden was interviewed by a local Las Vegas reporter after the trial. The smug reporter asked Rhoden, "Are you now willing to concede that it is a forgery?" Rhoden responded firmly. "Hell no. That verdict doesn't change the writing on the will. It doesn't change the evidence. True, I lost. I failed as a lawyer to convince a jury that the will was written by Howard Hughes. That was my fault. But my failure doesn't change the fact that the will was written by Howard Hughes. That will is genuine! I know it! I will always know it. And someday, perhaps, everyone will know it."

Now, the world knows it!